AF699936

Artificial Intelligence and Academic Integrity

Includes Connected Quizzing

STUDENTS, if your professor assigns Connected Quizzing associated with this book, please redeem the access code below, then enter the Class Code provided by your professor.

PROFESSORS, to assign Connected Quizzing for this book, please contact your Aspen Publishing representative. www.aspenpublishing.com/rep. They will assist you in setting up an account.

Your Connected Quizzing Access Code

Improve your learning outcomes through formative assessments with powerful reporting.

CasebookConnect.com/CQ

Scratch off with care.

Please note, after redeeming your access code, you will also be required to enter a **Class Code** provided by your professor.

10073145-0001

EDITORIAL ADVISORS

Artificial Intelligence and Academic Integrity

April G. Dawson
Associate Dean of Technology and Innovation
Professor of Law
North Carolina Central University School of Law

ASPEN
PUBLISHING

To contact Customer Service, e-mail customer.service@aspenpublishing.com, call 1-800-950-5259, or mail correspondence to:

Aspen Publishing
Attn: Order Department
1 Wall Street
Burlington, MA 01803

Printed in the United States of America.

1 2 3 4 5 6 7 8 9 0

ISBN 979-8-8890-6694-1

Library of Congress Cataloging-in-Publication Data

Library of Congress Cataloging-in-Publication Data application is in process.

About Aspen Publishing

Aspen Publishing is a leading provider of educational content and digital learning solutions to law schools in the U.S. and around the world. Aspen provides best-in-class solutions for legal education through authoritative textbooks, written by renowned authors, and breakthrough products such as Connected eBooks, Connected Quizzing, and PracticePerfect.

The Aspen Casebook Series (famously known among law faculty and students as the "red and black" casebooks) encompasses hundreds of highly regarded textbooks in more than eighty disciplines, from large enrollment courses, such as Torts and Contracts, to emerging electives, such as Sustainability and the Law of Policing. Study aids such as the *Examples & Explanations* and the *Emanuel Law Outlines* series, both highly popular collections, help law students master complex subject matter.

Major products, programs, and initiatives include:

- **Connected eBooks** are enhanced digital textbooks and study aids that come with a suite of online content and learning tools designed to maximize student success. Designed in collaboration with hundreds of faculty and students, the Connected eBook is a significant leap forward in the legal education learning tools available to students.
- **Connected Quizzing** is an easy-to-use formative assessment tool that tests law students' understanding and provides timely feedback to improve learning outcomes. Delivered through CasebookConnect.com, the learning platform already used by students to access their Aspen casebooks, Connected Quizzing is simple to implement and integrates seamlessly with law school course curricula.
- **PracticePerfect** is a visually engaging, interactive study aid to explain commonly encountered legal doctrines through easy-to-understand animated videos, illustrative examples, and numerous practice questions. Developed by a team of experts, PracticePerfect is the ideal study companion for today's law students.
- The **Aspen Learning Library** enables law schools to provide their students with access to the most popular study aids on the market across all of their courses. Available through an annual subscription, the online library consists of study aids in e-book, audio, and video formats with full text search, note-taking, and highlighting capabilities.
- Aspen's **Digital Bookshelf** is an institutional-level online education bookshelf, consolidating everything students and professors need to ensure success. This program ensures that every student has access to affordable course materials from day one.
- **Leading Edge** is a community centered on thinking differently about legal education and putting those thoughts into actionable strategies. At the core of the program is the Leading Edge Conference, an annual gathering of legal education thought leaders looking to pool ideas and identify promising directions of exploration.

This book is dedicated to my Dad, my favorite writer, walking partner, and biggest fan; and to my Mom, a caring and impactful educator for more than 25 years who continues to serve as my model even as she smiles down on me.

About the Author

April G. Dawson

Widely regarded as an expert on the role of technology in legal education, April Dawson is Associate Dean of Technology and Innovation and Professor of Law at North Carolina Central University School of Law, where she oversees the NCCU Technology Law & Policy Center.

Dean Dawson graduated *cum laude* from Howard University in 1994, where she was on the editorial board of the Howard Law Journal and a member of the National Moot Court Team. After law school, Dean Dawson joined the Civil Division of the U.S. Department of Justice, where she argued cases before the United States Courts of Appeals for the Fifth, Seventh, and Ninth Circuits. In 1996, Dean Dawson served as a law clerk to the Honorable Emmet G. Sullivan of the U.S. District Court for the District of Columbia, after which she joined a Washington, D.C., law firm as a litigation associate and was a legal writing adjunct at the George Washington University School of Law.

In 1999, Dean Dawson moved to North Carolina to start a private practice dedicated to representing employees in cases involving sexual harassment, discrimination, and related disputes. In 2006, she joined the faculty at NCCU and has taught a wide range of classes, including Artificial Intelligence and the Law, Legal Technology Equity and Leadership, Constitutional Law, Supreme Court Seminar, Torts, Administrative Law, and Voting Rights. Dean Dawson has been voted Professor of the Year multiple times.

Dean Dawson has presented several American Association of Law Schools (AALS) webinars such as Teaching with Technology for Maximum Student Engagement, Tech Productivity Tips for Law Faculty, and The Paperless Law Prof. She has served on the ABA TECHSHOW panels *Skills Building: Best Practices for Teaching Tech to Law Students*, and *Tech Forward: New Jobs for New Lawyers*. Dean Dawson was the recipient of the 2021 AALS Technology, Law and Legal Education Section Award, and was a 2022 ABA Women of Legal Tech Honoree. Dean Dawson's interest in technology can be traced back to her undergraduate degree in Computer Science from Bennett College and her work as a computer programmer prior to law school.

Dean Dawson is a member of the ABA Center for Innovation Governing Council, cohost of the ABA Innovation Network Podcast, vice chair of the North Carolina Bar Association Future of Law Committee, and immediate past chair of the AALS Section on Technology, Law and Legal Education. She is also a member of the North Carolina Governor's Task Force for Racial Equity in Criminal Justice, and vice chair of the Board of Directors for Democracy NC.

Dean Dawson cohosts Legal Eagle Review radio show with her colleague, Irving Joyner, on WNCU 90.7 FM, in which weekly interviews shed light on law-related concerns for people in the local community, as well as at the state and national level.

Contents

Chapter 2

Fundamentals of Academic Integrity

Chapter 3

Best Practices for Maintaining Academic Integrity in the Age of AI

Chapter 4

Use of Generative AI in the Legal Profession

Preface

Given my early background in computer programming, it is not surprising that I embraced the use of technology in my legal practice, and then again in my role as a law professor and associate dean. As a legal educator for almost two decades, I have long encouraged students to leverage technology to help them work smarter, not harder, and to enter the legal profession with the technology skills they need to practice law efficiently and effectively in the twenty-first century.

But as much as I endorse technology, I also understand the pitfalls and challenges that come with technological change. I am acutely aware that technology, if not designed, developed, and deployed responsibly, can further exacerbate discriminatory bias, causing continued harm to disadvantaged and marginalized communities. When teaching my students about the role of technology in the legal space, we often discuss these concerns.

In addition, the recent and rapid availability of generative AI tools to students presents positive opportunities for learning while also opening the door to potential misuse. Law students need assistance understanding the ethical implications of using generative AI tools in law school and in their future law practice. With *Artificial Intelligence and Academic Integrity*, I seek to offer law students that guidance and support.

Writing this book about generative AI and academic integrity—not even contemplated before the release of ChatGPT in November 2022—was a challenge, first because of the dynamic nature of generative AI technologies and tools; and second, because of the evolving response to generative AI in the legal education and practice landscapes. However, though the nature of technology and its impact are ever-changing, the principles of academic integrity and professional responsibility remain the same.

This book gives professors a vehicle for teaching students about the responsible use of generative AI. And it allows students to develop their professional identities as they delve into the academic integrity and professional responsibility implications of using generative AI. This book also encourages students to consider the societal and ethical implications of AI, the issues of AI governance, and the impact AI may have on the access to justice crisis.

To further engage students, I have integrated various features such as Professional Identity Formation Reflection questions, Examples, Case Studies, Exercises, informational sidebars, and QR codes that link to relevant sources. Designed to facilitate understanding and learning, these tools provide practical insights into real-world applications for AI technology and raise awareness of the challenges of using AI responsibly in the legal space.

It is my hope that *Artificial Intelligence and Academic Integrity* will serve as a key guide in your journey. I hope it will foster a meaningful and robust engagement with technology in your legal education and future practice.

Acknowledgments

This book would not have been possible without the support of many. Thank you to my most amazing support system, my kids—Alexander, Kari, Ayanna, and Andrew—for actively cheering me on and inspiring me every day with your adventurous spirits. I love you dearly.

Thank you to my dad, Richard Gordon, for confirming that I needed to write this book. Thank you to my sisters, brothers, and their beautiful families for their enthusiastic support and encouragement. Special thanks to my sister, Cyndela Walters, for being my accountability partner and hype woman.

Thanks to my wonderful student research assistants—Todd Ford and Caleb Williams. Your assistance and perspectives were invaluable.

Special thanks to Denise Clinton and Joe Terry from Aspen Publishing for your vision that brought this project to life and for your support, and to my editing team, Jessica Barmack and Jennifer Crane, who were incredibly helpful and who also burned the midnight oil alongside of me to get the project done.

Thanks to my colleagues at North Carolina Central University School of Law for their constant support, and special thanks to my NCCU Technology Law & Policy Center team colleagues for the work they do every day to help prepare our students for twenty-first-century practice—Diane Littlejohn, Cedric Pickett, Miriam Johnson, and Tim Cousin. And special thanks to my colleagues Kevin Lee and Nichelle Perry for their many contributions to the work of the Center.

Thank you also to Intel for supporting the NCCU Technology Law & Policy Center, especially Su Suh, Evangelina Almirantearena, Angel Preston, Jennifer Mancino, Katia Gondarenko, Lillian Yen, and Mike Haven.

Thank you to Siobhan Day Grady, with whom I teach AI Foundations and the Law, a class comprising her Masters of Information Science students and my law students. Who knew that teaching that class during the fall 2022 semester would lay a foundation for me to write this book? I look forward to teaching it again with you during the fall 2023 semester.

Thank you to all my students for being a source of inspiration for me. Special thanks to the students in my Summer I, 2023 Legal Technology Equity & Leadership (LTEL) class, which I taught while working on this book. Your enthusiasm and thoughtful observations, questions, and discussions gave me additional insight and energy as I worked on this project. And thank you to Dennis Kennedy, whose Legal Technology Leadership class inspired me to develop my LTEL course.

Thank you to the community of educators at all institutional levels who have, since the wide release of ChatGPT in November 2022, formed and organized academic integrity discussion groups, panels, and resources to assist teachers as we adapt to our rapidly changing educational environment.

Finally, I want to acknowledge the critical work being done in the responsible and ethical AI space by organizations like the Algorithmic Justice League, and the work being done in the Access to Justice space by organizations like the Institute for the Advancement of the American Legal System. I hope this book will plant seeds in our future lawyers so they will be leaders in helping to address these two vitally important areas.

A Note to Students

Professional Identity Formation Reflection Questions

In the past several months leading up to this book's publication, generative AI has become an increasingly prominent tool in the legal profession. However, in an academic setting, students' use of generative AI has raised concerns regarding potential conflicts with the principles of academic integrity—honesty, trust, fairness, respect, responsibility, and courage. As you navigate the appropriate use of generative AI in your legal studies, you also have an opportunity to consider those academic integrity principles in the context of ethical standards for legal practice and begin developing your professional identity as a lawyer.

While exploring artificial intelligence and academic integrity, this book also presents Professional Identity Formation Reflection questions. They are designed to encourage you to think critically about the material you have read and to reflect on how the concepts discussed relate to your values and aspirations and your understanding of what it means to be a lawyer.

Professional identity, as defined by American Bar Association (ABA) Standard 303(b)(3), is about understanding the special obligations you will hold as a lawyer toward your clients, colleagues, and society at large. Professional identity formation involves intentionally exploring the values, guiding principles, and practices for well-being that are foundational to success in legal practice.

Engage with these reflection questions openly and honestly. They are not merely academic exercises but opportunities for personal and professional growth. Consider them stepping stones on your way to becoming a lawyer with a strong sense of ethics, a deep understanding of the role of technology in the field of law, and a commitment to upholding the highest standards of professional integrity.

Remember, the journey of professional identity formation continues throughout and beyond law school, well into your legal career. I hope this book will help you gain valuable insights about the legal professional you want to become and will spark thoughtful reflection that will inform your path forward.

Chapter 1

Introduction to Artificial Intelligence

INTRODUCTION

Artificial intelligence (AI), particularly generative AI, is having a sudden and profound impact on the legal profession, as it is on virtually every profession across industries. In the practice of law, generative AI is being used to increase efficiency by augmenting and automating many legal tasks previously performed by lawyers or paralegals, such as legal research, drafting, and document review. Generative AI is also being used to develop new legal tools for predicting case outcomes, automating contract analysis, assessing risk, and providing legal advice.

As a result of this shifting landscape in the practice of law, it has become imperative for law students to learn about AI and to consider the educational and professional implications of these fast-paced and continually changing AI technologies. Indeed, as AI becomes an integral part of the legal profession, law firms, corporate offices, government agencies, and other legal employers will seek to hire lawyers who are tech-savvy. Understanding how to leverage AI tools appropriately will give law school graduates a competitive edge in the job market. As future lawyers, students will need to become adept at utilizing current AI technologies to enhance their efficiency and effectiveness.

Not only is generative AI changing the landscape of the legal profession, but it's also having a profound impact on the experience of students in law school. OpenAI's ChatGPT was released for general public use in November 2022, which made it available to students at all levels of education. Google and Microsoft have also deployed similar large language model (LLM) AI tools. Many students are now using these and other generative AI tools to assist with their coursework. This has significant implications for how and what students are learning, as well as for intellectual honesty and academic integrity.

Consequently, law students must develop a greater appreciation for the ethical implications of using AI in their education and recognize their responsibility to uphold academic integrity.

WHAT IS AI?

AI is a field of study in computer science that focuses on creating computer systems or programs capable of performing tasks that usually require human intelligence. These tasks might include understanding spoken or written language (e.g., Siri or Alexa or Grammarly), recognizing patterns in data (e.g., the recommendation system on Netflix), learning from experience (e.g., a self-driving car), or even making strategic decisions (e.g., game-playing computers such as AlphaGo and Deep Blue).

One of the best ways to conceptualize AI is to think about a computer that plays chess. The computer is trained on a large dataset of chess games and is able to "learn" strategies and tactics that have been used by human players. The computer uses algorithms (a set of rules or instructions) to determine the best moves based on the current state of the game.

> IBM's Deep Blue is a chess-playing computer that defeated world champion Garry Kasparov in a match in 1997.
>
> Google DeepMind's AlphaGo is a computer that can play Go, a complex board game that is considered by many to be even more difficult than chess. In 2016, AlphaGo defeated world champion Lee Sedol.

Another example of AI is when online shopping websites recommend products that seem to suit a shopper's tastes. To make good recommendations, the AI system analyzes past browsing and purchasing behavior and then predicts what may interest the shopper.

AI can also be used to analyze massive amounts of data and find patterns that would be too complex for a human to notice. For instance, AI can be used in health care to analyze patient data and help predict the likelihood of certain diseases.

In essence, AI is about designing computer systems that mimic human intelligence and capabilities to improve efficiency and solve complex problems. But as advanced as these systems are, it's important to remember that the current AI systems do not "think" in the same way humans do. AI uses mathematical principles to process data, make decisions, and learn from data. So, while it might appear that AI comprehends in the way humans do to perform human-like tasks, the processes employed by a computer are about math, patterns, and predictions.

It's also important to remember that although AI systems are becoming increasingly sophisticated, they are still not at the level depicted in movies such as *iRobot* and *Ex Machina*. That type of AI is called *artificial general intelligence*, or AGI. AGI[1] refers to systems that possess the ability to perform any intellectual task that a human being can do. These systems can understand, learn, adapt, and implement knowledge from one domain into another.

The type of AI used today, such as voice recognition, recommendation systems, or image recognition, is known as *narrow* or *weak* AI. And although ChatGPT has the ability to "learn" and generate human-like text across a wide range of topics, ChatGPT does not possess a broad or flexible understanding that can be applied across domains. For example,

> Since the launch of OpenAI's GPT API (Application Programming Interface, which allows other applications to interact with GPT models), companies and developers have been creating autonomous AI agents such as AutoGPT and BabyAGI. These applications can independently understand specific goals, create tasks to achieve those goals, execute the tasks, adapt priorities, and learn from their actions until the desired goals are reached. These applications are still in the early stages of development, but they show what may be the next step in creating AGI.

ChatGPT cannot drive a car. ChatGPT's capabilities are highly specific and limited to what it has been trained to do, that is, understand language and generate text. While generative AI may well be a stepping stone toward the creation of an AGI system, it's not sufficient on its own to achieve the full scope of capabilities associated with AGI.

AI SYSTEMS

To better understand the sophisticated and developing AI systems in wide use today, it's important to compare and contrast the two primary types of AI systems being used. The first type of AI system is *rule-based* (often called good old-fashioned AI, or GOFAI). Rule-based AI systems use a set of predefined rules to make decisions. The second major type of AI system is *machine learning*. These systems operate differently from rule-based AI systems as they "learn" from data rather than relying on explicit rules.

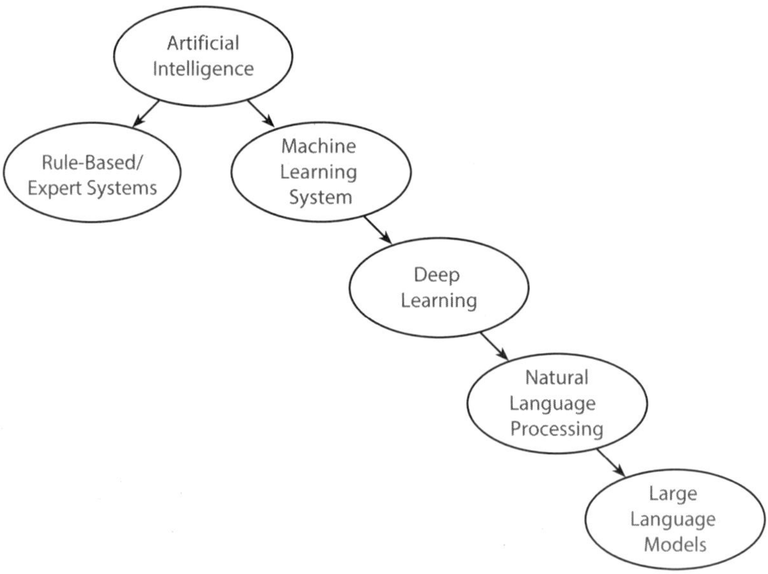

Figure 1.1 Artificial intelligence systems simple diagram.

Rule-Based AI Systems

Rule-Based AI

Rule-based or symbolic AI systems were the primary AI models used in the early days of AI development in the 1960s. Rule-based AI systems use a set of predefined rules to make decisions. They operate under the "if-then" principle; that is, if a certain condition is met, then the system will carry out a specific action.

An example of this type of rule-based AI is an automated customer service chatbot designed to answer commonly asked questions. In this system, some of the rules for the AI might look like this:

- If a customer asks, "What time do you open?," then the AI responds with, "We open at 9 A.M."
- If a customer asks, "What time do you close?," then the AI responds with, "We close at 5 P.M."

These rules guide the AI's decision-making process. When the AI receives an input ("What time do you open?"), it matches it to predefined rules like the ones above to produce output that corresponds to that rule ("We open at 9 A.M.").

Expert Systems

Another type of rule-based AI system is the *expert system*, also known as a *knowledge-based system*. These systems mimic the decision-making ability of a human expert. Expert systems include a knowledge base that contains a comprehensive set of rules and facts about a subject. These systems accept inputs (problems) from the user and provide outputs (solutions). Expert systems are used in various fields, such as medicine and finance, to help with tasks such as disease diagnosis and investment decisions. A simple example of a rule-based expert system would be one designed to help diagnose certain medical conditions based on the symptoms a patient is experiencing. This system's knowledge base — a set of rules and facts — might contain information like the following:

- If a patient has a high fever and a rash, they may have measles.
- If a patient has a high fever and a stiff neck, they may have meningitis.
- If a patient has chest pain and shortness of breath, they may have a heart condition.

When a patient comes in with a high fever and a rash, the symbolic AI expert system applies its rules to these facts, recognizes that these symptoms match the rule for measles, and then concludes that the patient may have measles.

Benefits and Limitations of Rule-Based AI Systems

Rule-based AI systems have several benefits. They allow experts to contribute their insights to these systems by creating rules that reflect their expertise and complex decision-making processes. Rule-based systems follow explicit "if-then" rules, making the reasoning and decision-making processes transparent, explainable, and easily understood by humans. This is important because it helps us understand how and why the AI system is making certain decisions. Rule-based systems give us the ability to trace the logic behind the AI system's actions, which is particularly valuable in fields where clarity and comprehension are crucial. By having clear rules that explicitly state, "if this condition is met, then take this action," we can ensure that the AI system's behavior is predictable and consistent. This predictability allows us to have greater control over the system and ensures it behaves in a reliable manner. Modifying or adding rules is straightforward, allowing for rapid adaptation to changing requirements or dynamic environments. Because they require less training data compared to other AI systems, they are more accessible and practical in situations where data may be limited or expensive to obtain.

However, despite these benefits, rule-based AI systems do have some limitations. One major disadvantage is that developing and maintaining rule-based AI systems requires significant time and effort. Creating rule-based systems involves experts and developers manually defining and encoding the rules, which can be a time-consuming and labor-intensive process. As the subject matter or information changes, the rules may need frequent modification or expansion, leading to ongoing maintenance efforts. This can also lead to scalability issues, as the number of rules can become difficult to manage in extremely complex systems.

Because rule-based systems strictly adhere to the predefined rules in a deterministic manner (meaning that when the system encounters a specific input, it will always trigger the same rule, leading to the same output), they lack agility and versatility in handling ambiguous or uncertain situations that require nuanced decision making.

Rule-based systems may also struggle with handling complex and high-dimensional data. They rely on explicit rules, which may not effectively capture intricate patterns or relationships in the data. Finally, rule-based systems cannot learn from new data or adapt to new situations unless human experts update their rules or facts. As a result, rule-based systems lack the flexibility and adaptability of machine learning models, which can adjust and learn from new data inputs, as discussed in the following section.

Machine Learning AI Systems

The second major AI system is machine learning. As we noted earlier, and unlike rule-based AI systems, machine learning systems can automatically learn and improve from experience without the need for explicit programming. In other words, machine learning systems can read and interpret data and use that data to learn for themselves.

Although AI research and development began in earnest in the 1950s, the development of machine learning–based AI systems stalled early on due to several challenges. One was that these systems require significant computational power, and, at the time, computing technology was still in its infancy. The computer processors of that era were not capable of handling the complex processing required for machine learning. Another major challenge was that machine learning requires large amounts of data to learn and make accurate predictions effectively, and during the early years, the necessary, vast, organized datasets were not readily available.

The 2000s saw rapid development in machine learning AI systems, largely the result of growth in two key areas: video gaming and the Internet.

The video gaming industry facilitated the advancement of AI because of the development of robust processors capable of managing the growing complexity of video games. When video games had simple 2D graphics, they didn't require much processing power. But as they became more complex, with 3D environments and high-resolution textures, their need for specialized processors increased dramatically, leading to the creation of graphics processing units (GPUs), designed to handle the intense workload of rendering graphics.

The powerful GPUs create the detailed and smooth graphics that make games so immersive. They do this by performing complex calculations simultaneously (as opposed to sequentially) to quickly generate the millions of pixels that make up each frame of the game. Without a powerful GPU, games wouldn't look as lifelike or play as smoothly as they do today.

The ability of GPUs to handle large parallel computer calculations made them ideal for training AI machine learning models. As mentioned, AI machine learning models rely on vast datasets and require extensive computational power to analyze the data and learn patterns from it. Traditional central processing units (CPUs), which are more general-purpose processors and perform calculations sequentially, are not as well-suited for handling the parallel computations required by AI machine learning models. GPUs offer specialized hardware that is optimized for handling the intensive computational demands of AI tasks. As a result, the use of GPUs significantly accelerated training times and allowed more complex AI models to be developed, leading to substantial advances in the field. Not surprisingly, manufacturers have started creating GPUs specifically tailored to AI tasks, reinforcing the crucial role of GPUs in AI research and applications.

The development of the Internet also played a big role in the development of machine learning systems. As mentioned above, machine learning models "learn" from analyzing large amounts of data. In this context, "learn" means identifying patterns and making predictions based on those patterns. The more diverse and plentiful the data the machine learning model can train on, the better the model can identify patterns, make predictions, and carry out tasks. The development of the Internet led to an explosion in data production and availability. Because data can be gathered from diverse Internet sources like social media and websites, an abundance of training material is available for machine learning algorithms to learn and refine their predictions.

There are, of course, other factors that led to the development of machine learning, such as advances in algorithms and the decreased cost of data storage. However, the increased processing power provided by GPUs and the substantial increase in training data made readily available by the Internet are two of the leading contributors to the advancement of machine learning AI.

How Machine Learning AI Systems Work

Before getting into the nuts and bolts of machine learning AI systems, let's take another look at the medical diagnosis AI system we mentioned earlier. What would a machine learning AI medical diagnosis system look like?

In contrast to a rule-based AI system, which relies on explicitly programmed rules about medical conditions to make predictions or decisions, an AI system using machine learning for medical diagnosis would "learn" to make predictions based on patterns it identifies in large amounts of data rather than by following explicitly programmed rules. The machine learning model would be provided with a comprehensive dataset consisting of patient records, symptoms, medical histories, and confirmed diagnoses. The system would then process and "learn" from this data, identifying relevant information. Machine learning algorithms would then map the relevant information to the corresponding diagnoses. After training, the AI model's accuracy would be evaluated on a new, unseen dataset before it would be employed for actual diagnostic predictions. Over time, the model would continue learning and improving accuracy by incorporating new patient data. Although these models learn, they are not perfect, and the outputs should always be reviewed by human experts.

As this example demonstrates, machine learning AI systems operate in a fundamentally different way from their rule-based counterparts. Rather than relying on a pre-set list of logical rules, machine learning models take in large quantities of data and draw inferences from it. With the power to compute a vast amount of data, machine learning systems may find patterns and relationships that even human experts might miss. However, it's important to remember that machine learning AI systems are not infallible. While these AI systems can analyze data at a scale that would be impossible for humans, AI predictions are only as good as the data their systems are trained on. And AI systems can't replace the experience, intuition, and judgment of humans. It's more accurate to think of machine learning AI as a tool to *augment* human expertise, rather than replace it.

Training AI

So, what is the mechanism for training machine learning AI models? One common example to help explain machine learning training is to imagine how children in school might learn to identify fruits. The teacher may ask them to look at several pictures of different fruits and then tell them what each picture represents. Over time, the students will learn to associate certain shapes, sizes, and colors with each fruit. Machine learning training works in a similar way.

AI developers provide the machine learning models with a lot of examples (data) with the correct answers (labels). The model then tries to understand the patterns or features that link the data with their corresponding labels. Once trained, the model can use what was learned to identify the correct label when the model is shown new data.

Machine learning training can be broadly classified into three types: supervised learning, unsupervised learning, and reinforcement learning. *Supervised learning*, as its name suggests, is like learning with a teacher. As in the example above, teaching the model to identify each fruit based on its characteristics, such as color, shape, and size, would be supervised learning.

Unsupervised learning is like learning through exploration. With unsupervised learning, the model is given data without labels, and the model tries to find patterns or structures within the data on its own. Returning to the fruit example, unsupervised learning would be like asking the model to group similar fruits together without telling it what each fruit is.

Reinforcement learning is like learning from trial and error or from rewards and penalties. A non-AI example of reinforcement learning is how you would train a dog. If the dog sits when you say "sit," you give it a treat (a reward). If it doesn't sit, it gets no treat (a penalty). Over time, the dog learns to associate the command "sit" with the action of sitting and learns to expect the treat as its reward for sitting.

In a similar way, a machine learning AI system trained using reinforcement learning will learn to associate *taking a particular action* with getting a reward. For example, the AI systems in autonomous cars are trained using a reinforcement learning algorithm, which learns by observing the vehicle's actions and the consequences. If the vehicle follows traffic rules, avoids collisions, and reaches its destination efficiently, it receives positive rewards (a high score). On the other hand, if it violates rules, causes accidents, or takes inefficient routes, it receives negative rewards (a low score). Over time, the algorithm learns the best driving policy that maximizes rewards (points), enabling the vehicle to make optimal decisions on the road.

> There is an emerging machine learning training model called *constitutional AI*. Developed by Anthropic A.I. and used to train its generative AI app, Claude, constitutional AI is an innovative approach in the field of artificial intelligence. It aims to create AI systems that align with a set of principles that guides their behavior. These principles operate like a constitution, ensuring that the AI system strives to be helpful, honest, and safe; avoids producing harmful or discriminatory outputs; and refrains from assisting in illegal or unethical activities.

Another example is the recommendation systems on streaming services that suggest personalized playlists to users. The algorithm learns by observing user interactions, such as listening duration, likes, skips, and playlist creation. If the algorithm suggests a song or television show that the user watches and likes, the model receives positive reinforcement. Conversely, if the suggestion is disliked or ignored, the model receives negative reinforcement. By learning from these feedback signals, the algorithm can improve its recommendations and tailor them to individual user preferences.

Deep Learning

As we have discussed, machine learning is a subset of AI that provides systems the ability to learn from data and to improve their performance without being *explicitly* programmed (like rule-based models). *Deep learning* is a subset of machine learning.

Deep learning works much like our brain does when we learn new things. At the heart of deep learning are structures called *artificial neural networks*, which are inspired by the network of neurons in the human brain. Like our brains, these networks take in a lot of data, learn to recognize patterns in this data, and gradually build a deep understanding of it. Deep learning is at the core of *large language models* (LLMs), such as OpenAI's GPT and Google's PaLM, which are discussed below.

Natural Language Processing

Before discussing LLMs and how they work, we need to first understand the broader field of *natural language processing* (NLP). NLP is a subfield

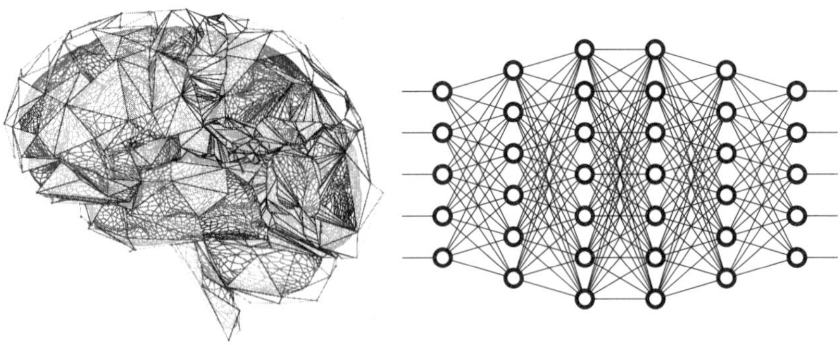

Figure 1.2 Deep learning neural net.

of artificial intelligence that focuses on the interaction between computers and human language. It involves programming computers to process, understand, and generate human language in a way that is both meaningful and useful to humans. And it's used in numerous applications, including translation services, sentiment analysis, chatbots, and voice assistants.

In its early stages, NLP primarily used rule-based methods (as we discussed in the section on Rule-Based AI Systems), where linguists manually defined sets of rules for the computer to follow when processing language. But these systems struggled with the complexity of human language. And with the development of machine learning and deep learning techniques, NLP systems became able to learn patterns from vast amounts of text data, which allowed them to handle the subtleties of language more effectively.

One of the most powerful tools used in NLP tasks is the LLM.

Large Language Models

Large language models are a type of generative AI. *Generative AI* is a subclass of artificial intelligence that focuses on generating new content, whether text, images, music, or computer code. Generative AI differs from traditional AI in that instead of just analyzing and making predictions about data, this model *creates new data* similar to the data on which it was trained.

For instance, a generative AI model could be trained on a dataset of images of cats, and it could then generate new images that look like cats but are in fact entirely unique—not identical to any image within the training dataset.

Large language models like GPT are also generative models that have been trained on a large corpus of text—they can generate human-like text based on their training.

Large language models are trained on large amounts of textbooks, articles, websites, and so on. As a result of the training, these models "learn" how language typically works, such as how sentences are structured and which words tend to follow others. They also learn to predict the next word in a sentence based on the previous words and can generate human-like text. They can write essays, answer questions, translate languages, and even write code.

However, it's important to note that while these models can generate impressive results, they don't *understand* the text in the way humans do. The model is simply *predicting* what word comes next based on patterns it learned from the data.

Following are brief descriptions of some of the major LLMs as of this writing.

> Although the general public became aware of GPT in November 2022, OpenAI has been working on its GPT large language models for several years. GPT-1 was released in June 2018. GPT-2, which improved on GPT-1 by increasing the model size and achieving better performance, was released in February 2019. GPT-3, which further improved on GPT-2 by scaling up the model size and introducing novel training techniques, was released in June 2020. These early models were available to researchers, developers, and businesses. GPT-3.5, which built on GPT-3 with additional fine-tuning and improvements, was widely released in November 2022. On March 14, 2023, OpenAI announced GPT-4, which in addition to being more advanced than GPT-3.5, is a large multimodal model that can accept image and text inputs to generate text outputs.
>
> To learn more, review OpenAI's research papers.

OpenAI — GPT, ChatGPT, and Bing

One of the most widely used LLMs is OpenAI's GPT (Generative Pre-trained Transformer). OpenAI's GPT language model became well-known when the company released *ChatGPT*, the chat interface or conversational AI that allows users to interact with the GPT models (GPT-3.5 and GPT-4).

When ChatGPT was first released in November 2022, it was

interfacing with GPT-3.5. That initial version of ChatGPT, which was free to use, reached one million users in its first five days and reached 100 million users in less than two months, making it the fastest growing app to date. In March 2023, OpenAI released its even more powerful GPT-4 LLM. Users could continue to use the free version of ChatGPT with access to GPT-3.5 or pay a monthly subscription and use ChatGPT to interface with GPT-4.

In February 2023, Microsoft, which has partnered with OpenAI, released *Bing Chat*, its AI conversational chat interface built on GPT-4.

Google—LaMDA, PaLM, and Bard

On May 18, 2021, Google announced at its Google I/O annual developer conference its *LaMDA* large language model. LaMDA (Language Model for Dialogue Applications) was built on the 2017 Google Brain–created Transformer models.

On April 4, 2022, Google announced *PaLM* (Pathways Language Model). During its May 2023 annual developer conference, Google announced the release of PaLM 2, second-generation version of its large language model.

On February 6, 2023, Google introduced *Bard*, Google's conversational AI chatbot, which is similar to ChatGPT. On March 21, 2023, a limited number of users were given early access, with others placed on a waitlist. Although Bard was originally powered by LaMDA, it's now powered by PaLM 2 and available for use by the general public without the need for a waitlist.

> In June 2022, Blake Lemoine, a software engineer at Google, claimed that LaMDA was sentient. Lemoine, who was working on the development of LaMDA, said he had been having conversations with the chatbot, and it had expressed feelings and opinions that he believed indicated sentience.
>
> Google has denied Lemoine's claims, saying that LaMDA is not sentient.

Meta — LLaMA

On February 24, 2023, Meta (formerly Facebook) announced the launch of its large language model, *LLaMA* (Large Language Model Meta AI). At the time of this writing, LLaMA is open source (providing access to Meta's source code, training data, and model weights) and currently available only to researchers. It also does not have a conversational chat interface like Bard or ChatGPT. However, Meta is expected to develop a commercial version of LLaMA and develop a conversational chat interface for LLaMA in the future.

• • •

There are other LLMs, including several open source LLMs, and new ones are being created at a rapid pace. However, before using any of the LLM tools available to the public, like ChatGPT, Bard, and Bing, it's imperative to understand their limits, to understand the academic integrity implications, and to ensure that you use them in a way that facilitates and not thwarts your law school learning and development. Additionally, all students, but especially law students, should advocate for responsible and ethical AI.

ETHICAL AND RESPONSIBLE AI

AI brings with it an assortment of ethical concerns, including privacy issues, discriminatory biases, and lack of accountability. As future lawyers, judges, and legislators, law students should be mindful of the societal risks associated with AI.

When AI systems process vast amounts of data, they can inadvertently invade individuals' privacy by accessing, analyzing, and utilizing personal information without explicit consent. AI models can also inadvertently reflect and propagate harmful biases present in the training data, leading to discriminatory outcomes that exacerbate social inequalities. Additionally, the lack of transparency of AI algorithms, often called "black boxes," can hinder explainability and accountability, making it difficult to identify and rectify sources of error or bias.

The United States does not have comprehensive legislation regulating the development and deployment of AI, leaving gaps in addressing privacy concerns, biases, and the lack of transparency.[2] Without clear regulations, individuals' privacy can be compromised, discriminatory outcomes can persist, and the legal implications of AI decisions become uncertain. To ensure responsible and accountable AI practices, it's crucial for policymakers to enact comprehensive laws that promote transparency, consent, fairness, and explainability. Such legislation would safeguard privacy rights, mitigate biases, and enable individuals and organizations to assess the legitimacy and ethical implications of AI-generated outcomes.

Explainable AI (XAI) refers to the ability to understand and justify the reasoning behind AI systems' decisions or predictions. Without explainability, it becomes challenging to evaluate the fairness, reliability, and legality of AI-generated outcomes. Without explainability and transparency, users of and those impacted by AI systems will not have the necessary trust and confidence in those systems.

There are several governmental agencies and non-governmental organizations (NGOs) that promote ethical AI through policies and initiatives. Governmental agencies include:

- *National Artificial Intelligence Initiative*: This initiative is led by the White House Office of Science and Technology Policy (OSTP). It aims to accelerate the responsible development and use of AI in the

On May 16, 2023, the Senate Judiciary Subcommittee on Privacy, Technology, and the Law, held a three-hour hearing on Oversight of A.I.: Rules for Artificial Intelligence. Witnesses were Samuel Altman, CEO, OpenAI; Christina Montgomery, Chief Privacy & Trust Officer, IBM; and Gary Marcus, Professor Emeritus, New York University.

United States. The initiative includes a number of ethical principles that should guide the development and use of AI, such as fairness, transparency, accountability, and privacy.

- *National Institute of Standards and Technology (NIST)*: NIST is a federal agency that develops and promotes measurement, standards, and technology. NIST has developed guidelines for the development and use of AI, including a framework for assessing the ethical implications of AI systems. On June 22, 2023, the U.S. Secretary of Commerce Gina Raimondo announced that NIST is launching a new public working group on AI to address the rapid changes in the technology.
- *Department of Defense (DoD)*: The DoD is responsible for the national security of the United States. The DoD has developed ethical principles for the development and use of AI in defense applications, including protecting human rights, avoiding bias, and ensuring that AI systems are used in a responsible manner.

Prominent NGOs working on ethical and responsible AI include:

- *Partnership on AI (PAI)*: PAI is a nonprofit organization that brings together leaders from academia, industry, and government to work on the safe and beneficial development of artificial intelligence. PAI has published a number of reports on the ethical implications of AI, and it has developed a set of principles for the development and use of AI systems.
- *Center for Human-Compatible Artificial Intelligence (CHAI)*: CHAI is a research center at Stanford University that focuses on the ethical and social implications of artificial intelligence. CHAI works to develop new approaches to AI that are aligned with human values, and it supports research into the potential risks and benefits of AI.
- *Institute for Ethics & Emerging Technologies (IEET)*: IEET is a nonprofit organization that promotes public understanding of the ethical implications of emerging technologies. IEET publishes a journal, hosts conferences, and produces educational materials on a range of emerging technologies, including AI.

- *Algorithmic Justice League (AJL)*: AJL is a nonprofit organization that works to combat the harms of algorithmic bias. AJL conducts research on algorithmic bias, and it advocates for policies and practices that can reduce bias in AI systems.
- *Center for Artificial Intelligence and Digital Policy (CAIDP)*: CAIDP is a nonprofit research organization that is dedicated to promoting the responsible development and use of artificial intelligence and digital technologies. CAIDP was founded in 2020 by a group of experts from academia, industry, and government who are concerned about the potential risks of AI and digital technologies.
- *Distributed AI Research Institute (DAIR)*: DAIR is a nonprofit research organization that was founded in 2021. DAIR is dedicated to conducting research on the ethical and social implications of AI. DAIR is also committed to developing new approaches to AI that are aligned with human values. DAIR is a community-rooted organization, and its work is informed by the lived experiences of its members. DAIR's team is composed of researchers, organizers, and activists from across North America, Europe, and Africa.

As AI technology continues to move at a rapid pace, policymakers need to stay proactive and adaptive in addressing the evolving ethical challenges it presents. As future policymakers and leaders in the legal community, law students have a crucial role to play in shaping the ethical and regulatory landscape of AI. You must stay informed about the latest developments in AI technology and its potential ethical implications.

ENDNOTES

1. AGI is also called *general, broad,* or *strong* AI.
2. Although there are U.S. policy statements on AI, such as the White House Blueprint for an AI Bill of Rights released in October 2022, and the announcement by the Biden-Harris administration on May 4, 2023, on new actions to promote responsible AI innovation that protects Americans' rights and safety, the United States does not have comprehensive legislation for regulating the development and deployment of AI (see https://www.whitehouse.gov/briefing-room/statements-releases/2023/05/04/fact-sheet-biden-harris-administration-announces-new-actions-to-promote-responsible-ai-innovation-that-protects-americans-rights-and-safety/).

Chapter 2

Fundamentals of Academic Integrity

INTRODUCTION

Lawyers are not just advocates—you (as future lawyers) are also advisors, negotiators, and intermediaries who are relied on to act with honesty, fairness, and professionalism. A lawyer's ability to effectively fulfill these roles is largely dependent on the level of trust they can build and maintain. That is why it is crucial for you, as an aspiring practitioner, to develop a thorough understanding of academic integrity, how it shapes your legal educational journey, and how it continues through to your practice of law.

In this chapter, we delve into the meaning, importance, and application of academic integrity in legal education before looking at strategies for maintaining academic integrity in the age of AI.

WHAT IS ACADEMIC INTEGRITY?

Academic integrity is the ethical commitment to being truthful in your scholarly and educational work, and it is one of the cornerstones of all institutions of higher education. The International Center for Academic

Integrity defines academic integrity as a commitment to these six fundamental values:[1]

1. *Honesty*, the first of the six values of academic integrity, entails consistent truthfulness and sincerity in all scholarly pursuits. It demands a commitment to producing original work, appropriately attributing sources, and avoiding any form of misrepresentation.
2. *Trust* fosters an environment where you are assured that your work will be appraised impartially and where institutional rules and standards will be respected.
3. *Fairness* mandates consistent application of clear guidelines, ensuring you are all assessed using the same criteria.
4. *Respect* involves recognizing and acknowledging others' efforts and contributions, thus encouraging cooperation and collaboration.
5. *Responsibility* is recognizing one's role in upholding academic integrity, reporting infractions, and accepting the repercussions of violations.
6. *Courage* involves upholding these values under challenging circumstances where it might be tempting to adopt easier routes.

Understanding and appreciating these six values are prerequisites to practicing academic integrity. Students, educators, researchers, and administrators are expected to embody these values in all facets of academic life.

Professional Identity Formation Reflection

Take a moment to think about the values of academic integrity: honesty, trust, fairness, respect, responsibility, and courage. Imagine what an educational environment would look like where everyone upholds these values. Reflect on your past educational experience. Did the school you attended have such an environment? Why or why not?

Reflect on whether you upheld the academic integrity values as a student at your previous educational institutions. In the context of your future legal career, how do these values contribute to your professional identity as a future lawyer?

WHY IS ACADEMIC INTEGRITY IMPORTANT?

As previously noted, academic integrity, while vital in all areas of education, holds particular significance in law schools because principles of honesty, trust, fairness, respect, responsibility, and courage align closely with the professional ethics expected of lawyers. Additionally, academic integrity plays a pivotal role in learning, assessing your knowledge and abilities, fostering a culture of trust, and developing respect for intellectual property.

Academic Integrity Facilitates a True Reflection of Your Knowledge and Abilities

When you uphold the principles of academic integrity, you are committing to produce work that is truly your own, and the work you produce is a genuine manifestation of your understanding and the skills you have developed. Thus, one of the most important reasons academic integrity matters is that it allows for a true reflection of your knowledge and abilities.

Academic integrity enables law school faculty to accurately gauge what you have learned, how well you understand it, and how well you can communicate what you have learned. Being able to truly appraise your work not only helps educators evaluate your progress accurately, it also helps *you* understand your own strengths and areas for improvement.

You can only get a true picture of your intellectual growth when your academic conduct aligns with your principles of academic integrity.

In the context of legal studies, a field that hinges on fine-tuned analysis and critical thinking, academic integrity ensures that the legal arguments you craft, the case analyses you conduct, and the interpretations of statutes and case law you propose are truly your own. This work output not only reflects your understanding of the law but also your ability to apply it—a key skill for any aspiring lawyer. Without academic integrity, a student's work product cannot be accurately measured, hindering the objective of legal education to produce skilled and ethical legal practitioners.

Metacognition

Metacognition is an awareness of your own knowledge—what you do and do not know—and an awareness of your own learning process—the best strategies for your unique way of learning. For example, when you practice metacognition, you will intentionally and actively (1) assess your understanding of a subject, (2) identify areas of weakness, (3) employ a specific study plan using techniques that help you learn, and (4) monitor your learning of the subject.

Moreover, having one's actual work assessed facilitates a growth mindset. Law school's rigorous and challenging nature demands resilience, adaptability, and an unwavering commitment to learning. A growth mindset transforms your challenges into opportunities for growth and learning. It also helps you persevere during setbacks and handle criticism effectively.

A *growth mindset*, introduced by psychologist Carol Dweck, is a psychological theory that suggests an individual's abilities and intelligence can be developed through dedication, hard work, and a love for learning. This is in contrast to a *fixed mindset*, where individuals believe their talents and skills are set in stone. People with a growth mindset are more inclined to embrace challenges, persist in the face of challenges, and view effort as a path to mastery. They are also better able to learn from criticism and find lessons and inspiration in the success of others.[2]

This mindset supports healthier mental states and promotes more effective learning strategies.

A growth mindset remains important as law students transition into their professional careers as lawyers. With the legal field's dynamic and evolving nature, lawyers must constantly learn and adapt. Lawyers with a growth mindset handle setbacks effectively, use criticism for self-improvement, find creative solutions to problems, and strive to offer better service to clients. This mindset cultivates curiosity and encourages lawyers to tackle new challenges, laying the groundwork for ongoing professional growth.

Professional Identity Formation Reflection

Reflect on the relationship between academic integrity, a growth mindset, and your professional identity formation. How do you believe upholding academic integrity will shape your growth mindset in your legal education and future legal practice? How can the principles of academic integrity help foster a resilient and adaptable approach to your legal studies and future career? In what ways do you believe a growth mindset could impact your ability to innovate and improve as a legal professional? How can both academic integrity and a growth mindset contribute to your ongoing professional development and ability to serve clients effectively?

Academic Integrity Facilitates Authentic Learning

Academic integrity and authentic learning are deeply intertwined concepts, each facilitating and reinforcing the other in various educational fields, including legal studies. Academic integrity, at its core, promotes the creation and preservation of original, genuine work, pushing you to engage with your studies on a profound level. Such an approach requires a deep interaction with the material, pushing you to not merely read or memorize but to understand, critique, and form your own insights.

Authentic learning is the approach to education that emphasizes real-world, practical applications of knowledge and skills. Applying what you learn in the classroom to real-life scenarios facilitates your legal education by fostering critical thinking, legal reasoning, and decision-making skills, all of which are essential for future lawyers. Authentic learning is of paramount importance in law school because law is a dynamic and practical discipline, deeply intertwined with societal realities. Authentic learning requires that you not merely memorize legal statutes, but that you also understand and apply them within diverse and complex real-life situations.

In law school, through clinics, intern- and externships, moot court and client counseling competitions, and other experiential learning opportunities, you practice applying theoretical knowledge to real-world scenarios, which is key in shaping you into an adept legal professional. These experiences not only enhance your understanding of legal principles and theories but also equip you with practical skills such as negotiation, advocacy, and problem-solving. Thus, authentic learning in law school bridges the gap between theory and practice. It fosters a deep, holistic understanding of the law and its application, ultimately preparing you to practice law.

Thus, the practice of academic integrity sets the stage for authentic learning because it promotes the kind of intellectual engagement and critical thinking that authentic learning seeks to achieve.

Professional Identity Formation Reflection

Think about the legal learning experiences you have had that were most impactful. Did these experiences involve applying your knowledge to real-world situations or circumstances? Would the learning experiences have been as meaningful if you did not have the necessary foundational knowledge? Would the learning experiences have been as meaningful if you were not fully engaged?

In the context of your future legal career, how will an authentic learning experience in law school impact your ability as a future lawyer to continue to learn and stay abreast of developing law?

Academic Integrity Fosters a Culture of Trust

Law is a profession grounded in trust, and this trust is cultivated from the earliest stages of legal education. By upholding academic integrity, you not only validate your own learning but also lay the foundations for a professional culture that highly values trustworthiness, honesty, and ethical behavior.

Adherence to academic integrity in law school nurtures a culture of trust by demonstrating a commitment to honesty and transparency. When you produce work that is truly your own, you showcase your respect for original thought, the ideas of others, and the intellectual process itself. You demonstrate that you can be trusted to engage with legal principles, analyze complex cases, and make interpretations in an honest and responsible manner. Such practices send a clear message that you are not just competent, but also reliable, thus building trust with your professors and peers.

This culture of trust, fostered by academic integrity, is crucial in the practice of law. The legal profession is built on a foundation of trust and ethical conduct, principles that are deeply embedded within the tenets of academic integrity. The culture of academic integrity in law school is intended to prepare you to become a trustworthy professional, one who upholds the high ethical standards of the legal profession.

Professional Identity Formation Reflection

Reflect on how your commitment to academic integrity could contribute to fostering a culture of trust within your law school. How does demonstrating academic integrity signal trustworthiness, honesty, and ethical behavior to your professors and peers?

What are the potential impacts of this culture of trust on your future legal practice? What are the ways in which a culture of trust, established through academic integrity, could influence your approach to your professional relationships and responsibilities in the legal field?

Academic Integrity Develops Respect for Intellectual Property

The study of law includes exposure to intellectual property rights, such as copyrights, patents, trademarks, and trade secrets. As a future practitioner of law, you will need to understand, respect, and uphold these intellectual property concepts. Adherence to academic integrity ensures that respect for the intellectual property of others is ingrained in your legal education.

Law school requires you to acknowledge the sources of your ideas and avoid plagiarism, a practice that demonstrates respect for intellectual property. When you properly cite sources, you are recognizing and validating the original thought, effort, and creativity behind the ideas or work of others. This not only aligns with the ethical standards of academia, it also mirrors the principles that govern intellectual property law in the wider world. Hence, by practicing academic integrity, you are learning to appreciate the value of other people's intellectual contributions, an essential skill for your future career.

Professional Identity Formation Reflection

Reflect on how your practice of academic integrity can contribute to your understanding and respect for intellectual property rights. How does acknowledging sources and avoiding plagiarism demonstrate respect for the intellectual work of others?

How can this practice prepare you for your future legal career, particularly in areas related to intellectual property law? How does practicing academic integrity help you appreciate the value of other people's intellectual contributions and how can this respect influence your professional conduct in your future legal career?

Academic Integrity Lays the Foundation for Professional Ethics

As we shall discuss more fully in the following sections, academic integrity in law school lays the groundwork for the ethical conduct that will be expected of you in the legal profession, which is one that demands a high standard of ethical behavior.

Lawyers are entrusted with significant responsibilities. They often deal with sensitive information, represent clients in very personal matters, and make decisions that can have far-reaching consequences. For these and other reasons, adherence to professional ethics, including honesty, confidentiality, and respect for the law, is absolutely essential. By cultivating these same values in law school, you will be better prepared to uphold them in your legal career.

Professional Identity Formation Reflection

Reflect on the connection between academic integrity and professional ethics in the practice of law. How does upholding academic integrity prepare you to uphold professional ethics in your legal career?

ACADEMIC INTEGRITY AND THE ETHICS OF THE LEGAL PROFESSION

As you transition from academia into the legal profession, you will discover that the principles of academic integrity apply equally to ethical standards for legal practice. The core academic integrity values of honesty, trust, fairness, respect, responsibility, and courage, discussed in the beginning of this chapter, will continue to guide your behavior, decision making, and professional conduct within the legal community.

Here are the six values discussed in the context of a lawyer's professional responsibility:

1. *Honesty* in the legal profession will require truthfulness in all your interactions—with clients, with the court, and with opposing counsel. As a lawyer, you will be obligated to accurately represent the law, provide sincere advice, and refrain from making knowingly false declarations.
2. *Trust* involves your maintaining client confidentiality and affirming trust in the legal system by adhering to the rule of law.
3. *Fairness* involves representing your clients adeptly and zealously without using legal procedures in unethical ways to disadvantage your opponents.
4. *Respect* is exhibited by treating all participants in the legal process with dignity, avoiding discrimination, and recognizing the legal rights of all individuals.
5. *Responsibility* extends beyond your duty to your client. As a lawyer, you are responsible for upholding the law and the standards

ABA *Model Rules of Professional Conduct* provide standards of legal ethics and professional responsibility for lawyers in the United States. Several of the rules relate to the values of honesty, trust, fairness, respect, responsibility, and courage. Here are some examples:

Rule 1.6 —Confidentiality of Information

Rule 3.3 —Candor toward the Tribunal

Rule 3.4 —Fairness to Opposing Party and Counsel

Rule 4.1 —Truthfulness in Statements to Others

Rule 4.4 —Respect for Rights of Third Persons

Rule 5.1 — Responsibilities of Partners, Managers, and Supervisory Lawyers

Rule 8.3 —Reporting Professional Misconduct

of the legal profession, maintaining the confidence and secrets of your clients, and serving the broader public interest. You are also responsible for monitoring your own ethical conduct as well as reporting any unethical behavior you observe in the profession.

6. *Courage* for a lawyer embodies standing up for ethical values, even when faced with adversity or when it might be more profitable to circumvent those values.

In essence, legal ethics extend the principles of academic integrity into the realm of legal practice, ensuring a seamless transition from academic to professional ethics. By ensuring you develop an understanding of, respect for, and adherence to academic integrity values, law schools can help ensure that future lawyers uphold the values of the profession.

DISSECTING ACADEMIC DISHONESTY

While you are undoubtedly aware of some of the conduct that constitutes academic dishonesty, it is worth delving into the varied behavior that may give rise to academic integrity issues. It is also critically important for you to understand why students may engage in academic dishonesty and be supplied with suggestions for avoiding such behavior.

Types of Academic Dishonesty

Academic dishonesty manifests in several forms, each undermining the fabric of academic integrity in its unique way.

Plagiarism

Plagiarism involves using someone else's work or ideas without proper attribution, effectively presenting their work as your own. In the context of law school, this could involve copying legal arguments from another source; using uncited excerpts from judicial opinions, legal journals, or textbooks; or submitting a legal brief or essay that is not entirely your own work. Plagiarism not only undermines your learning process, it also violates the principles of honesty and respect.

Essentially, with plagiarism, you rob yourself of the opportunity to engage in authentic learning. Moreover, plagiarizing disrespects the intellectual labor that someone else put into their original work; it infringes on their intellectual property rights. Hence, plagiarism in law school is a form of academic dishonesty that stands in stark contrast to the principles of academic integrity and professional ethics that legal education seeks to instill.

Cheating

Cheating in law school involves dishonest actions that a person takes to gain an unfair advantage. It may manifest in various forms, such as using unauthorized resources during examinations, sharing answers with peers, or submitting work as your own that was in fact done by someone else.

In the context of legal education, cheating fundamentally undermines your learning process. It creates a false impression of your abilities and knowledge, thereby defeating the purpose of assessments, which is to accurately gauge your understanding and competency. More importantly, cheating breaches the trust between you, the faculty, and your peers. In the legal profession, such actions can damage or even destroy your reputation, which can have long-lasting effects, as we shall discuss in more detail later.

Unfair Advantage

A form of academic dishonesty, unfair advantage involves actions that give you, as a student, an improper edge over your peers, and it is a significant issue in law schools. Such actions can range from gaining unauthorized access to examination questions beforehand or submitting false excuses to delay exams or assignments to using technology dishonestly during closed-book exams. By creating an unequal playing field, these actions disrupt the equitable academic environment that law schools strive to maintain.

In essence, by gaining an unfair advantage, you contradict the principles of fairness and respect that are integral to academic integrity. Moreover, these actions distort the accurate assessment of your learning. Needless to say, engaging in these practices conflicts with the ethics and professional responsibility expected of future legal practitioners. Unfair advantage is a form of academic dishonesty that is fundamentally incompatible with the principles and objectives of law school.

Facilitating Academic Dishonesty

Facilitating academic dishonesty is another form of academic misconduct, which, although less obvious than plagiarism or cheating, is equally problematic, especially in the context of law school. This involves helping or enabling others to commit acts of academic dishonesty, such as giving them answers during exams, completing assignments on their behalf, or knowingly allowing others to plagiarize your work.

While some of you may not see this as a form of academic misconduct, given that you may not directly benefit from the dishonest act, facilitating academic dishonesty is a fundamental breach of integrity. It contributes to a dishonest academic environment, and it undermines the learning process of the person whose dishonesty was facilitated.

Moreover, in a profession that places a high premium on ethics and integrity, facilitating dishonest practices contradicts the values of honesty, responsibility, and fairness that are expected of future legal professionals. Consequently, you should understand that enabling other students to engage in academic misconduct is a serious violation of academic integrity, one that runs counter to the fundamental principles that underpin legal education and practice.

Understanding the Causes of Academic Dishonesty and Suggestions for Avoiding Such Behavior

As you work your way through law school toward a profession anchored in ethical practice and public trust, understanding the causes of academic dishonesty is not only imperative, but it also provides an opportunity for self-reflection and personal growth. By examining the reasons that lead some individuals to engage in academic dishonesty, you can interrogate your own motivations and behaviors and allow yourself to acknowledge your own potential vulnerabilities. When you understand the factors that can push people toward academic dishonesty—such as high levels of stress, the desire for success, peer influence, or lack of understanding of the rules[3]—you are better positioned to identify and resist those same temptations. You can actively seek out appropriate resources, support, and strategies to maintain your integrity, even in challenging circumstances. Take this as an opportunity to work toward strengthening your commitment to academic integrity.

When you understand the factors that contribute to academic dishonesty, you can contribute to a culture of integrity within your educational community. You can engage in conversations about these issues, help raise awareness, challenge behaviors that normalize dishonesty, and advocate for fair policies and supportive resources.

So why do some students find themselves contemplating and succumbing to academic dishonesty?

High Academic Pressure

Law school is known for its intense, competitive environment. You often face significant pressure to perform well and stand out in a demanding curriculum. In some cases, this high-pressure environment can push you to resort to dishonest means to achieve your academic goals. To combat this, strive to focus on your own learning and development instead of comparing yourself to others. Remember that your worth is not defined by your grades, but by your growth and understanding of the law.

Fear of Failure

The fear of failing or not meeting academic expectations can drive you to engage in academic dishonesty. This fear may stem from personal standards, parental expectations, or perceived future career prospects. Some of you may believe that achieving high grades, even through dishonest means, outweighs the risk of being caught. To address this, remember that it's okay to ask for help when you're struggling. Reach out to your professors, peers, or academic support professionals. They can provide guidance and reassurance, which can significantly reduce the pressure you feel.

Inadequate Preparation or Poor Time Management

If you feel inadequately prepared for your coursework or struggle with time management, you may resort to academic dishonesty to meet deadlines or cope with challenging assignments. To combat this, work on developing solid study habits and time-management skills. Your law school academic support office can be especially helpful in assisting you in devising a study schedule to help you better manage your time. Don't wait until you have an issue. Be proactive and schedule a meeting with one of your school's academic support professionals at the beginning of each semester.

Perceived Unfairness

Perceptions of unfairness or inconsistency in grading, perceived favoritism, or a belief that others are cheating without consequence can also lead you to justify dishonest behavior. You may see it as a way to level the playing field in a system you view as unjust. If you feel that grading is inconsistent or unfair, consider discussing your concerns with your professors or academic advisors rather than resorting to dishonesty. Don't let the bad behavior of others sway you from your commitment to academic integrity. Maintaining your honesty, even in the face of unfairness or perceived inequality, is integral to your personal and professional growth. It's important to remember that achieving success by sticking to principles of honesty and integrity may be challenging, but it is ultimately more rewarding and commendable.

Peer Influence

The behavior and attitudes of peers can significantly influence a student's actions. If academic dishonesty is prevalent or normalized within your student community, individuals may be more likely to engage in such behaviors, viewing them as acceptable or necessary to keep pace with your peers. Be the change you wish to see. Uphold academic honesty in your work, and advocate for it among your peers.

Lack of Understanding

Another cause is the lack of understanding or awareness about what constitutes academic dishonesty. You or your peers may unintentionally engage in dishonest behaviors, such as plagiarism or inappropriate collaboration, simply because you are not fully aware of the academic integrity policies or how to properly cite sources. Make sure you familiarize yourself with your law school's academic integrity policies and guidelines. If you're unsure about proper citation or collaboration practices, don't hesitate to ask your professors or use resources provided by your institution.

The Influence of Technology

With the expanding availability of online resources, the opportunity for academic dishonesty has increased. You may be tempted to misuse these resources by plagiarizing from online sources, or accessing unauthorized material during online examinations. While using these resources for studying and understanding is beneficial, be cautious not to misuse them, especially when it comes to plagiarism or unauthorized assistance during online examinations. Moreover, with the proliferation of technology tools, you may unintentionally cross the line while using these tools without fully understanding the ethical implications.

• • •

Understanding why you might be tempted to engage in conduct that is contrary to academic integrity will help you take proactive and intentional action to better respond to circumstances that are triggering. Also, understanding the causes of academic dishonesty carries significant professional implications. Lawyers often find themselves in high-stakes, high-pressure situations, and understanding the factors that can lead to dishonesty may help you navigate these professional challenges with integrity. The skills and values you develop in the process of understanding and combating academic dishonesty—such as seeking assistance when needed—are transferable to your future role as a legal professional.

Professional Identity Formation Reflection

Reflect on the causes of academic dishonesty discussed in this section. How do these factors resonate with your own experiences and challenges? How can understanding these causes help you strengthen your commitment to academic integrity?

Consider ways to mitigate these pressures and temptations in your own academic journey. How can you use resources, support systems, and personal strategies to maintain integrity in the face of these challenges?

Reflect on how these experiences in law school can prepare you for future challenges in your legal career. How can understanding the causes of academic dishonesty and practicing integrity help you navigate high-stakes, high-pressure situations with honesty and integrity? What support resources for lawyers can you leverage to ensure you uphold professional ethics in your legal practice?

Law School Consequences of Violating Academic Integrity

Just as it is important to understand why students might engage in academic dishonesty, it is also important for you to be clear about the consequences when a student violates academic integrity standards. Academic dishonesty is taken seriously in institutions of higher learning, including law schools. Consequences of engaging in such behavior can vary widely depending on the nature and severity of the violation, the policies of the specific institution, and whether it is a first-time or repeated offense. Following are some potential formal disciplinary actions and other consequences that could result from academic dishonesty.

Warning or Reprimand

In some cases, especially for first-time offenses that are less severe, a student may receive a formal warning or reprimand. This serves as an official notice that the student's behavior has violated the school's academic integrity policy, and it usually comes with the implication that further violations will result in more severe consequences.

Failing Grade or Zero on the Assignment

A common penalty for academic dishonesty is receiving a failing grade or a zero on the assignment on which the violation occurred. This action can significantly impact a student's overall grade in the course.

Failing Grade for the Course

In more serious cases, a student may receive a failing grade for the entire course, regardless of their performance on other assignments or exams. This could considerably delay a student's academic progress, affect their scholarship eligibility, or even affect the immigration status of international students.

Academic Probation

Academic probation is a severe consequence that usually lasts for a specified period, during which you are expected to demonstrate integrity in all your academic pursuits. Any violations during this period may result in more serious consequences, such as suspension or expulsion.

Suspension

In serious cases of academic dishonesty or in situations where the student has repeatedly violated the academic integrity policy, the student may be suspended. This means that they are temporarily prohibited from attending the university and taking classes.

Expulsion

The most severe consequence for academic dishonesty is expulsion from the institution. This is usually reserved for the most egregious offenses or for repeated violations after previous disciplinary actions. Expulsion is a permanent dismissal. A student who is expelled may find it difficult to gain admission to other academic institutions.

Notation on Academic Transcript

Some institutions may place a notation on a student's academic transcript indicating academic dishonesty. This can affect their chances of getting admitted to other academic programs, or even their employment prospects, as the transcript serves as an official record of their academic performance and conduct.

Damaged Academic Reputation

In addition to the formal disciplinary actions discussed above, academic dishonesty damages a student's reputation. This tarnished reputation might affect the student's relationships with faculty and peers.

Moreover, you may not fully appreciate that the reputation you build in law school will follow you as a legal professional, and a tarnished reputation will impact future career opportunities.

> *Compromised Reference Letters:* Obtaining letters of reference from law professors is necessary for law students for several endeavors. Professors are less likely to provide strong, positive reference letters if you are known to have engaged in academic dishonesty. A lack of compelling references can impede your prospects when applying for internships, clerkships, post-graduate studies, and employment.

> *Impaired Peer Relationships:* Establishing strong relationships with your law school classmates, which begins on your first day of law school, is vitally important. Your classmates will provide valuable and necessary support throughout your law school career. Academic dishonesty can lead to mistrust and resentment among your peers, which can be detrimental to your relationships. Collaborative activities such as group projects or study groups may be affected, and your peers may be less willing to share resources, engage in discussions, or offer support. Moreover, your law school peers are your future professional colleagues, and the reputation you build in law school will follow you as a legal professional.

• • •

Embracing academic integrity ensures a healthier, more authentic academic experience and fosters the development of trustworthy and ethical legal professionals.

Professional Consequences of Violating Academic Integrity

Just as there are immediate and far-reaching consequences of engaging in academic dishonesty in law school, this behavior also has significant professional consequences.

Challenges in Bar Admission

As you know, the journey to becoming a lawyer culminates in seeking a license to practice law. The bar application process typically involves two crucial steps: First, you must demonstrate your comprehensive understanding of the law by passing the bar exam, and second, you must exhibit the character and fitness required to practice law. This character and fitness evaluation seeks to protect both the public and the justice system by ensuring applicants possess the moral integrity needed for the practice of law.

Bar admission committees conduct character and fitness evaluations, and a history of academic dishonesty can be a serious red flag. The consequences of a damaged academic reputation can extend to difficulties in obtaining professional licensure.

The American Bar Association and National Conference of Bar Examiners' Code of Recommended Standards for Bar Examiners identifies academic misconduct as one of the major factors in the character and fitness evaluation. Among the 56 states and jurisdictions that evaluate applicants, academic misconduct is widely recognized as extremely pertinent.[4]

Employment Obstacles

Prospective employers, particularly in the field of law, value integrity highly. Academic dishonesty can raise questions about your professional ethics, which may affect your employability or advancement within a law firm or other legal entity.

• • •

Rebuilding your reputation after academic dishonesty can be a long, challenging process. It requires demonstrating a commitment to integrity, honesty, and ethical behavior over time, and even then, some opportunities may be permanently lost. Therefore, it's essential to uphold academic integrity at all times to preserve your academic reputation and ensure a fruitful career in the field of law.

Personal Consequences of Violating Academic Integrity

Academic dishonesty carries not just external consequences, such as disciplinary actions and damaged reputations, but also personal and psychological impacts. In the following sections, we delve into the personal consequences and negative effects on mental health that can stem from engaging in academic dishonesty.

Erosion of Self-Esteem

Engaging in academic dishonesty often results in a significant erosion of self-esteem. As you resort to dishonest means to achieve your goals, you may start doubting your own capabilities and competence. This diminished self-confidence can become a self-perpetuating cycle, leading to increased reliance on dishonest practices and further diminishing self-esteem.

Increased Anxiety and Stress

Engaging in academic dishonesty can cause you to experience heightened levels of anxiety and stress. The fear of being caught, the guilt associated with dishonest actions, and the pressure to maintain a facade of achievement can create a constant state of worry. This chronic stress can contribute to a range of physical and mental health problems, from sleep disorders and headaches to depression and anxiety disorders.

Loss of Trust in Self

Trust in one's own abilities and moral compass is crucial to personal development. Academic dishonesty undermines this trust, as you may begin to feel that you cannot succeed without resorting to dishonest means, or you may feel guilty and conflicted about your actions.

Impaired Moral and Ethical Development

Academic integrity is closely tied to personal integrity, which forms the basis for ethical behavior in your professional and personal life. Engaging in academic dishonesty can impede moral and ethical development, as it reinforces the idea that dishonest behavior is a viable means to an end. This can create difficulties in making ethical decisions in the future, in both personal and professional contexts.

Implications on Personal Relationships

Academic dishonesty, and the associated guilt and loss of self-trust, can also affect your personal relationships. It can lead to a fear of being discovered, difficulty in trusting others, or a tendency to be dishonest in personal interactions.

• • •

These personal consequences can extend beyond the academic realm. Doubts about your own competence, chronic stress, and impaired moral judgment can negatively impact your professional life. They can hinder your job performance, contribute to workplace stress, and compromise your professional ethics. The scope and reach of these consequences underscore the importance of maintaining academic integrity while you're in law school. It's essential, not just for academic and professional success, but for your personal well-being, too.

Support services, such as counseling or mental health services, are often available at academic institutions for students struggling with these issues. Many state bars also provide free resources for law students.

Professional Identity Formation Reflection

Reflect on the range of disciplinary actions that could result from academic dishonesty in law school. How do these potential consequences influence your understanding of the seriousness of such violations? Reflect on the concept of an academic reputation. How does academic dishonesty tarnish this reputation, and what are the potential long-term impacts?

The consequences of academic dishonesty extend into the legal profession, particularly in the bar admission process. Reflect on how a history of academic dishonesty could impact your path to becoming a lawyer.

Consider the implications of academic dishonesty in your personal life. How can engaging in such behavior affect self-esteem, stress levels, self-trust, moral and ethical development, and personal relationships? Reflect on the role of support services in helping students navigate the pressures and consequences of academic dishonesty. How can you utilize these resources in your own academic journey?

Considering all the potential consequences of violating academic integrity, how are you motivated to uphold academic integrity in your studies? What strategies will you employ to ensure your actions align with this commitment?

Examples: Violations of Academic Integrity and Their Consequences

The following scenarios illustrate the pitfalls of violating academic integrity and the rewards of upholding it, even in difficult situations.

> *Example 1*: A law student was found to have copied substantial portions of her final paper from a legal article she found online, failing to give due credit. Upon discovery, the student was reported to the academic integrity board, faced a failing grade, and was suspended for the following semester. This infraction was added to her academic record, which was later reviewed by the bar, putting her admission into question.
>
> *Example 2*: In a high-stakes law exam, a student was caught with cheat sheets containing answers to potential questions. His actions were reported to the law school disciplinary committee, resulting in an immediate failure in the exam, a mark on his academic record, suspension for a semester, and loss of trust from his professors and peers.

These realistic scenarios underscore both the immediate and long-term consequences of violating academic integrity. Such misconduct jeopardizes not only your academic standing and future career prospects, but also your relationships and reputation.

Professional Identity Formation Reflection

Reflect on the two scenarios provided. How could these students have acted differently to uphold academic integrity, even under pressure? What lessons can be learned from these scenarios about the importance of maintaining academic integrity as part of your professional identity formation? How might these scenarios influence your own approach to academic work and professional conduct?

Examples: Upholding Academic Integrity in Difficult Situations

As future lawyers, you must strive to act ethically, even when the path is challenging.

> *Example 1*: A law student noticed a classmate cheating during an exam but was torn about reporting it, fearing potential backlash. Recognizing her duty to uphold academic integrity, she reported the incident to the professor. Her action was praised by faculty, reinforcing the importance of honesty and courage in maintaining academic integrity.
>
> *Example 2*: During a moot court competition, a law student had the chance to use confidential information about the opposing team's strategy, which she had accidentally come across. Despite the temptation, she chose not to use it, valuing fairness over a potential win. Her action, revealed after the competition, earned her respect from her peers and faculty alike.

Professional Identity Formation Reflection

Reflect on the first example where a law student noticed a classmate cheating. What emotions and thoughts would you experience if you were in her position?

What values and professional obligations guided her decision to report the cheating incident to the professor? Reflect on the significance of her actions in terms of professional identity formation.

Reflect on the second example where a law student had access to confidential information about the opposing team's strategy. What ethical considerations would you have if you were in her position?

How did her decision to not use the confidential information demonstrate her professional identity and integrity? Reflect on how her actions might have influenced her peers' perception of her.

How can these scenarios guide your own professional identity formation as a future lawyer? Reflect on any personal experiences that have shaped your professional ethics.

Case Studies: Professional Responsibility and Ethical Obligation

These cases demonstrate the complex intersection of personal, professional, and ethical obligations. They provide a valuable look at how the values of academic integrity (honesty, trust, fairness, respect, responsibility, and courage) translate to situations involving lawyers' professional and ethical responsibilities.

Case Study: Mata v. Avianca, Inc. (Part I)

Mata v. Avianca, Inc., a case filed in the Southern District of New York, was a personal injury case in which plaintiff Roberto Mata sued the airline Avianca, claiming that he was injured when a metal serving cart struck his knee during a flight to John F. Kennedy International Airport in New York. Counsel for the defendant, Avianca, filed a motion to dismiss. Plaintiff's counsel, Peter LoDuca, filed an opposition to a motion to dismiss with citations to cases the defendant's counsel could not find. When the defendant's counsel called this to the court's attention, the court issued an order requiring Mr. LoDuca to provide

> an affidavit annexing copies of the in-question judicial opinions cited in his opposition to the motion to dismiss. Mr. LoDuca submitted an affidavit on April 25, 2023, providing citations and attaching copies of court opinions cited in the opposition to a motion to dismiss and declaring that the information in the affidavit was true and correct. However, six of the submitted cases were fabricated by ChatGPT. LoDuca submitted a subsequent affidavit on May 25, 2023, admitting that he did not conduct the research or verify the cases he declared to be true and correct in his April 25, 2023, affidavit. The court ordered LoDuca to show cause why he shouldn't be sanctioned for the use of a false and fraudulent notarization in his affidavit filed on April 25, 2023.

LoDuca's April 25, 2023, submission was not only in violation of legal ethics and professionalism, but it also misled and violated the trust of the court and opposing counsel. His actions undermined the legal process and disrespected the principles of truthfulness, honesty, and fairness that underpin the legal profession. Further, LoDuca's submission of an affidavit attesting to the veracity of cases, which proved bogus, amounted to perjury, a criminal offense.

For you, this case highlights the non-negotiable requirement for absolute integrity in all aspects of your future practice. It underscores the necessity of conducting thorough, accurate legal research and the duty of honesty owed to the court and other legal practitioners. The fact that LoDuca chose to bypass these principles resulted in potential legal and professional consequences, damaging his reputation and credibility in the process.

Mata v. Avianca, Inc. (also discussed in more detail in Chapter 3), serves as a stark reminder that the legal profession is built on a foundation of trust, and every action a lawyer takes, whether in or out of court, should be grounded in honesty and respect for the law. This case further underscores that academic integrity goes beyond the classroom, extending into every part of a legal professional's work. As such, you must internalize the importance of honesty, accuracy, and thoroughness in your work. The consequences of breaching these principles, as evidenced in this case, can be career-altering.

Professional Identity Formation Reflection

Reflect on the actions of Peter LoDuca in the case. What ethical principles did LoDuca violate in his handling of the case? Consider the values of academic integrity (honesty, trust, fairness, respect, responsibility, and courage) in your answer. How might LoDuca's actions impact his professional relationships and reputation in the legal community?

The case underscores that academic integrity extends into every part of a legal professional's work. Reflect on how this understanding influences your approach to your studies and future legal practice. What lessons can be learned from this case about the importance of honesty, accuracy, and thoroughness in legal practice? How will you apply these lessons in your future career as a lawyer?

Case Study: *The North Carolina Ninth Congressional District Election Fraud Investigation Hearing (2018)*

The 2018 general election in North Carolina's Ninth Congressional District was a contest between Democrat Dan McCready and Republican Mark Harris. Although Harris appeared to win by a narrow margin, the North Carolina State Board of Elections (NCSBE) twice refused to certify the results of the race because of potential irregularities involving mail-in ballots. The NCSBE launched an investigation into allegations of fraud in the handling of absentee ballots. It was alleged that a political operative working for Harris, Leslie McCrae Dowless, had collected and potentially tampered with absentee ballots, a practice known as "ballot harvesting," which is illegal in North Carolina.

The NCSBE held an evidentiary hearing in February 2019. Mark Harris had stated publicly several times that he knew nothing about any illegal activity being done on behalf of his campaign. However, on February 20, 2019, John Harris, Mark Harris's son and an assistant U.S. attorney in North Carolina, testified that he had repeatedly warned his father not to hire Dowless because Dowless appeared to have previously engaged in illegal tactics to win votes. Harris presented emails and phone records as evidence, contradicting his father's claims that he had no prior knowledge of any wrongdoing.

On February 21, the board unanimously voted to call a new election because of fraud by Republican operatives. Mark Harris, citing health issues, chose not to run in the subsequent election.

John Harris found himself in an extraordinarily difficult position when he became aware of potentially illegal activities in his father's political campaign. John Harris's decision to testify against his father, despite the deeply personal implications, underscored his commitment to uphold the truth and the rule of law, reflecting the essence of academic integrity.

This case underscores the principle that integrity, the pursuit of truth, and the upholding of ethical standards should always supersede personal and professional affiliations. As future legal professionals, you are expected to uphold the highest standards of academic integrity. Just like John Harris, you must be prepared to make tough decisions that prioritize truth and justice even when personal relationships or interests are at stake.

Professional Identity Formation Reflection

Imagine you were in John Harris's position, finding out about potentially illegal activities in a close family member's campaign. What steps would you take and why?

In this case, Harris chose to testify against his father, a deeply personal decision. Reflect on a time when you faced a similar dilemma where personal relationships conflicted with your professional obligations. How did you navigate this situation?

This case underscores the importance of integrity, truth, and ethical standards. As a future legal professional, how would you ensure that these values are maintained in your practice, especially when faced with difficult decisions?

Reflect on a time when you had to stand up for what you believed was right, even if it went against popular opinion or the views of those close to you. What did you learn from this experience?

• • •

While navigating the legal landscape, you must remember that your actions reflect not only on your personal character but also on the wider legal profession. These cases serve as stark reminders that maintaining academic integrity is not merely about avoiding plagiarism or cheating on exams but encompasses broader ethical considerations about honesty, accountability, and the rule of law.

ENDNOTES

1. International Center for Academic Integrity (ICAI), *The Fundamental Values of Academic Integrity*, 3d ed. (Albany, NY: International Center for Academic Integrity, 2021). https://academicintegrity.org/images/pdfs/20019_ICAI-Fundamental-Values_R12.pdf.
2. Carol Dweck, *Mindset: The New Psychology of Success* (New York: Ballantine Books, 2016).
3. See Donald L. McCabe, Kenneth D. Butterfield, and Linda K. Treviño, *Cheating in College: Why Students Do It and What Educators Can Do about It* (Baltimore, MD: Johns Hopkins University Press, 2012).
4. Claire Guback and Judith Ann Gundersen, eds., Code of Recommended Standards for Bar Examiners, *Comprehensive Guide to Bar Admission Requirements* (ABA/NCBE, 2023).

Chapter 3

Best Practices for Maintaining Academic Integrity in the Age of AI

Having already discussed the foundations of both AI and academic integrity, in this chapter we discuss best practices for maintaining academic integrity in the Age of AI.

SHOULD YOU USE GENERATIVE AI IN LAW SCHOOL, OR SHOULD IT BE BANNED?

Using generative AI such as ChatGPT in an academic setting poses several ethical and practical challenges. You may be wondering whether you should use generative AI at all in law school. Indeed, at least in the early days of ChatGPT's release, some law school professors and administrators suggested that generative AI tools should be banned altogether. However, as educators at all levels have learned more about the technology, it is now generally accepted that a ban is not tenable for several reasons.

First, large language models (LLMs) such as ChatGPT are widely accessible and are being integrated within applications widely used by law students, such as Google and Microsoft products. In the near future, generative AI assistance in Microsoft Word and Google Docs will be as commonplace as spellcheck and grammar check, making banning generative AI impractical. Also, because of the ease of access, prohibiting the use of generative AI will not prevent its use, and it is practically impossible to reliably detect its use.

In addition to the impracticability of having an absolute ban, there are several pedagogical reasons for allowing the use of generative AI and incorporating responsible use of it in the learning process. As discussed more fully later in the chapter, generative AI tools, such as ChatGPT, can be valuable educational aids when used responsibly. They can help you understand complex legal concepts, generate ideas for legal arguments, and prepare for exams. The key is to ensure that you use these tools to enhance your learning, not to replace your own work or to gain an unfair advantage.

Banning the use of generative AI in law school would also deprive students of the opportunity to learn and adapt to these emerging technologies, which are becoming essential tools in the legal profession. The task of legal educators is to ensure that students are instructed on the ethical and responsible use of these tools. And it is your responsibility as a law student and future lawyer to understand these tools, adhere to academic integrity when using them, and develop the judgment needed to use them in legal practice.

BEST PRACTICES WHEN USING GENERATIVE AI IN LAW SCHOOL

Having determined that it is impractical and undesirable to completely ban generative AI tools from law school, let's delve into the best practices for maintaining academic integrity while utilizing generative AI tools. This chapter will discuss how generative AI technologies can be used responsibly and ethically to augment, not undermine, your learning.

Understand Academic Integrity Rules at Your Institution

Of course, the first step in avoiding engaging in academically dishonest behavior is to know what that behavior looks like. As discussed in Chapter 2, academic dishonesty can take many forms, from plagiarism and cheating on exams to unauthorized collaboration and unfair advantage. However, impermissible conduct, particularly conduct involving the use of generative AI, can vary from one institution to another, from one course to another, and even from one assignment in the same course to another. Therefore, you must understand the specific policies and expectations at your school and for your individual courses.

Virtually all law schools have a comprehensive academic integrity policy that outlines what constitutes academic dishonesty and the consequences of violating that policy, as required by the American Bar Association (ABA) (or other accrediting body). The Program of Legal Education chapter in the ABA Standards and Rules of Procedure for Approval of Law Schools provides in relevant part as follows:

> Standard 301. OBJECTIVES OF PROGRAM OF LEGAL EDUCATION (a) *A law school shall maintain a rigorous program of legal education that prepares its students, upon graduation, for admission to the bar and for effective, ethical, and responsible participation as members of the legal profession.* (b) A law school shall establish and publish learning outcomes designed to achieve these objectives.

> Standard 302. LEARNING OUTCOMES *A law school shall establish learning outcomes that shall, at a minimum, include competency in the following*: (a) Knowledge and understanding of substantive and procedural law; (b) Legal analysis and reasoning, legal research, problem-solving, and written and oral communication in the legal context; *(c) Exercise of proper professional and ethical responsibilities to clients and the legal system; and (d) Other professional skills needed for competent and ethical participation as a member of the legal profession.*

Additionally, Standard 308 requires that law schools publish a code of conduct:

> Standard 308. ACADEMIC STANDARDS (a) *A law school shall adopt, publish, and adhere to sound academic standards, including*

> *those for regular class attendance, good standing, academic integrity, graduation, and dismissal.*
> (b) A law school shall adopt, publish, and adhere to written due process policies with regard to taking any action that adversely affects the good standing or graduation of a student.

The *ABA Standards and Rules of Procedure for Approval of Law Schools*, Chapter 3 — Program of Legal Education.

To know what is expected of you in terms of academic honesty, you should thoroughly read and understand your law school's *code of conduct*. A law school's code of conduct will also explain the consequences of engaging in academically dishonest behavior.

In addition to the institution-wide policy, your professors may have their own policies regarding academic integrity. These policies may be included in their course syllabus, or your professor may explain their policy in class. You must pay close attention to these policies, as they may provide more specific guidelines about acceptable and unacceptable behavior in that particular course.

Understanding these standards of conduct has always been vital, but even more so now that powerful generative AI tools are available. You need to fully appreciate that while generative AI can assist your learning process, its misuse can lead to breaches of academic integrity. And, as discussed in Chapter 2, the consequences of academic dishonesty will impact your academic career and have serious implications for your professional reputation in the future.

By fully comprehending what constitutes academic dishonesty in law school, by understanding the consequences of such behavior, and by committing to your own academic integrity, you lay a foundation for an ethically sound legal career.

Exercise

Locate your law school's academic integrity policy, often available on the institution's website or in the student handbook. What are the specific behaviors that are considered violations of this policy? How could these behaviors potentially occur in your academic journey? What steps do you plan to take to ensure you avoid these violations and uphold principles of academic integrity?

Professional Identity Formation Reflection

Reflect on your understanding of your law school's academic integrity policies, especially in relation to the use of generative AI tools. How do these policies shape your approach to using AI in your studies? Can you recall a situation where you had to decide about using an AI tool for a task? How did you navigate that situation, and what did you learn from it?

How do these experiences, and your commitment to upholding academic integrity, contribute to your professional identity as a future lawyer?

Understand the Privacy Implications of Using ChatGPT and Other Generative AI Tools

As with any digital tool, you must understand the privacy implications of using generative AI applications such as ChatGPT. Before using these tools, ask yourself the following questions:

- What data is being collected?
- How is the data being processed?
- Is my data being stored?

- Is my data being used for AI training?
- Is my information being shared with third parties and third-party vendors?
- What steps do they take to protect my privacy when shared with third parties?

This is not an exhaustive list. The only way to know the answers to these and other important privacy-related questions is to carefully read and understand the privacy policies and terms of service of the AI tool you are using. The privacy policies and terms of service will typically answer these questions and more.

You need to take steps to protect your own privacy. As you use generative AI and other digital tools, remember, do not input your *personally identifiable information* (PII) or any sensitive or confidential information. It is also good practice to regularly review and update your privacy settings and to stay informed of any changes to the privacy policies or terms of service for the digital tools you use.

You must protect other people's information as well. If you are in a clinic, you need to be especially cautious about client confidentiality. Do not share any personally identifiable or sensitive information about your clients while using unsecured AI tools. (As discussed in Chapter 4, some legal technology companies have deployed generative AI tools on secure servers and keep information confidential.) Entering confidential client information into unsecured generative AI systems could lead to breaches of attorney-client privilege and confidentiality. There is also a risk that information shared with a generative AI tool could become part of the training data for the AI model, potentially further exposing confidential client data.

Understanding the privacy implications of using generative AI tools is especially critical for you, as one who will soon be entering a profession where client confidentiality and data security are paramount and will be part of your ethical and professional responsibilities. Using generative AI tools in a responsible way that respects and safeguards your privacy and the privacy of others while you are in law school supports your personal security, protects your clinic clients' information, and prepares you for future practice.

Exercise

Read the privacy policies for the following generative AI tools.

OpenAI ChatGPT

Privacy Policy

Terms of Use

Google Bard

Google Privacy Policy

Google Terms of Service

Generative AI Additional Terms of Service

Generative AI Prohibited Use Policy

Microsoft Bing

Privacy Statement

Terms of Use

Professional Identity Formation Reflection

Think about how you would maintain client confidentiality while leveraging the benefits of these technologies. How might you approach educating yourself about privacy policies and terms of service?

Consider scenarios where you might need to make decisions about using digital tools in light of these privacy considerations. How do you foresee these decisions impacting your professional conduct and the development of your legal practice?

Understand the Appropriate Uses of Generative AI as a Tool

Since the release of ChatGPT to the general public in November 2022, generative AI has been a transformative force in many sectors of society, including the legal profession and legal education. And while generative AI has the potential to augment research, streamline case preparation, and provide insights into complex legal concepts, it should be emphasized that AI is a *tool*—no more, no less. A calculator can be used to accelerate computations, but it should not replace your understanding of the underlying mathematical principles. Similarly, generative AI may be appropriate in law school to assist in some academic work, but it should not replace the intellectual engagement necessary for true learning and academic growth. You must remember that the purpose of law school is to foster your understanding of complex legal concepts and to help you develop the skills of critical thinking and effective communication. Generative AI can be a valuable tool in helping you achieve these goals, but the intellectual labor, growth, and development must be your own.

Below are some suggestions for how you might use generative AI tools appropriately in law school. However, you should always confirm with your professors that your use of generative AI is appropriate.

To Help You Understand Legal Terminology

Large language model conversation chat tools such as ChatGPT can be used as an interactive legal dictionary. Learning legal vocabulary, which includes unfamiliar terminology that represents complex concepts, may be one of the most challenging aspects of law school for new students. You can use generative AI large language models to find definitions of legal terms or concepts in easy-to-understand language.

You can also engage in a dialogue with language models. In real time, you can ask follow-up questions to clarify your understanding of terms and concepts, which can reinforce learning and ensure that you fully understand the terminology.

Language models can also break down complex legal phrases or sentences into simpler language and explain what each part means. They can also provide examples of how specific terms are used in sentences or legal documents.

While these methods can be very effective in helping you understand legal vocabulary, it's important to remember that AI models such as ChatGPT are tools to *supplement* learning. They should not replace traditional learning methods such as reading legal texts, attending lectures, participating in class discussions, and conferring with your professors.

You can find a sample ChatGPT "Legal Terminology" dialogue here:

Additionally, the information provided by AI should always be cross-checked with authoritative legal sources for accuracy.

To Help You Understand Complex Topics

Another major challenge of law school is the complexity of the topics that you need to master. AI language models can assist you by providing plain-English explanations of legal principles and explaining complex legal concepts in simpler terms, making the material more accessible. You can also engage in interactive Q&A sessions with language models to help clarify your understanding of legal topics. You can ask an interactive language model tool specific questions about the topic you're studying and get immediate responses. This can be particularly helpful when you are studying independently and do not have immediate access to a professor or a peer. AI language model tools can also provide summaries of significant court cases and highlight the key points of a case, the legal principles applied, and how the decision impacts existing laws or precedents.

Again, any legal interpretations provided by AI should be cross-checked with authoritative sources. You must always read the authoritative source. You should also remember that some AI tools, such as ChatGPT, may not be able to provide the most recent updates beyond their last *training cutoff date*, meaning, they do not have access to more recent or real-time information after that date, so results may not include the latest legal developments or changes in the law.

> You can find a sample ChatGPT "Complex Topics" dialogue here:

To Help You Prepare for Exams

Preparing for exams, especially during the first year of law school, can be daunting, as law school exams differ significantly from exam formats used in college. Conversational large language models can be a useful tool when you prepare for your exams. You can use language models to generate practice questions on specific legal topics. By answering these questions, you can check your understanding of the material and get a sense of the types of questions you might encounter on the exam. Large language models can also help you prepare study plans and suggest effective study strategies.

While ChatGPT can be a very useful tool for exam preparation, it's important for you to remember that it's not a replacement for thorough study and review. Also, any information provided by ChatGPT should be cross-checked with reliable sources, and you should seek help from your professors and academic support offices if you are struggling with your preparation.

You can find a sample ChatGPT "Exam Prep" dialogue here:

To Assist You with Legal Research and Writing

You need to develop exceptional legal research and writing skills to become a competent lawyer. The law is composed of statutes, case law, and regulations, and your ability to gather relevant sources, interpret their significance, construct logical arguments, and apply legal principles to actual scenarios is heavily reliant on your research and writing capabilities.

AI has been used by the two most popular and comprehensive digital legal research platforms, LexisNexis and Westlaw, for decades. However, until recently, the primary type of AI utilized by these platforms was predictive AI, that is, AI that uses algorithms and machine learning to predict the relevance of a document. With the recent and rapid development of large language models and generative AI, these platforms are beginning to offer more robust generative AI assistance, such as document analysis, document summarization, and document drafting.

While the use of these robust generative AI tools is wholly appropriate for practicing lawyers, you should be able to conduct independent research, critically analyze legal principles, and produce sound legal writing yourself *before* relying on generative AI tools to accelerate your process. Law school is designed to help you develop these skills, which are integral to a successful legal career.

You can gain a nuanced understanding of the law by actively engaging in independent research and analyzing cases, statutes, and secondary legal sources. You must also learn to evaluate legal authorities, weigh conflicting arguments, and employ logical reasoning when crafting your written work. Relying prematurely on generative AI will inhibit your development of key research and writing skills, which are honed through trial and error.

Moreover, legal writing is a skill that requires practice and refinement. Writing is an iterative process, which means that a piece of work undergoes several drafts and revisions before it reaches its final form. The first draft is rarely perfect; each subsequent draft allows for refinement of ideas, clarification of arguments, and improvement in language and style. In legal writing, this iterative process is essential to develop a clear, persuasive, and legally sound argument. Generative AI should not be relied on to bypass this crucial stage of honing legal writing skills. It is through engaging in this process that you not only improve your writing but also gain a deeper understanding of the law and its application.

Once you have developed strong, independent research and writing skills, using generative AI tools in legal research platforms in a manner consistent with your school's code of conduct may be appropriate. Without a doubt, the addition of generative AI in legal research platforms such as LexisNexis and Westlaw allows for a more efficient research process. After you have fully developed your independent research skills, generative AI functionality can help you to sort through and comprehend the vast amounts of information available, quickly identify relevant authority, and gain insights that can improve your understanding of complex legal concepts. Moreover, by assisting with tasks such as document analysis and summarization, the generative AI tools in the legal database platforms can save you time and allow you to focus on critical thinking and crafting persuasive legal arguments.

While AI may be valuable in helping you find relevant law, legal research includes the ability to analyze, interpret, and apply the law. This cannot be outsourced to AI. AI is there to assist in the research process, not replace the vital analytical and interpretative skills that form the foundation of competent legal practice.

Professional Identity Formation Reflection

As you consider your development as a law student, think about a specific instance where you were tempted to rely on generative AI to assist with a complex legal research or writing task. Why were you tempted to use AI in this situation?

Reflect on your decision and the eventual outcome. Did you choose to rely on your own skills, or did you use AI? How did this choice impact the final result and your learning?

Considering this experience, how do you view the balance between developing your own abilities and using technological aids such as generative AI? How might this balance factor into your development as a future lawyer?

Understand the Limitations of AI

As seen in recent news stories and discussed in this book, ChatGPT can provide inaccurate or fabricated information, including fake cases and legal opinions. Although lawyers have begun using generative AI tools to draft documents, they need to fully appreciate the limitations of those tools.

Likewise, as a law student, you must first understand how large language models work and their limitations before using generative AI tools. As discussed in Chapter 1, while generative AI models can generate impressive text, these models do not "understand" information in the same way humans do. You must consult original sources to confirm that the information you are receiving from generative AI tools is factual.

ChatGPT Sometimes Provides False Information

ChatGPT, despite its remarkable capabilities, can occasionally produce responses that contain false or fabricated information.[1] Understanding why this might occur can help you use generative AI tools more responsibly.

ChatGPT may produce false information because its responses are generated based on patterns and associations it has learned from vast amounts of training data, primarily derived from the Internet. The data includes diverse sources, ranging from reputable legal resources to unverified content. Consequently, ChatGPT's responses can reflect biases, inaccuracies, or misinformation that was present in the training data. Moreover, as mentioned above, generative AI models, such as ChatGPT, have a training data cutoff date. As the law evolves and new legal developments emerge, AI models such as ChatGPT may not be able to incorporate these updates into their responses until new and updated data are provided.

An AI model's output is only as good as the data on which it was trained. If an AI model has not been trained on specific data or if that data is incorrect, outdated, or biased, the AI's output will reflect these limitations.

Garbage in, garbage out (GIGO) is a popular phrase used in computer science and information technology. GIGO expresses the idea that the quality of the input determines the quality of the output. If you put inaccurate, inappropriate, or low-quality data into a system (the "garbage in"), the system will produce inaccurate, inappropriate, or low-quality results (the "garbage out"). This concept is particularly relevant in the context of AI and machine learning training.

ChatGPT Sometimes Hallucinates

In addition to sometimes providing false information, ChatGPT sometimes *fabricates* information or *hallucinates* and generates hypothetical scenarios, fictitious precedents, or opinions that are not grounded in real legal authority. This can happen because ChatGPT is not capable of contextual understanding in the same manner as a human, meaning that ChatGPT cannot grasp the nuances, implications, or consequences of different legal situations or arguments. ChatGPT also cannot distinguish between facts and opinions, or between reliable and unreliable sources of information.

ChatGPT uses statistical patterns and probabilities from its training data to generate responses. In other words, the model's responses are based on patterns identified in the training data, rather than on a comprehensive grasp of legal principles. When the generative AI model is asked for information beyond its training data, or in contexts that require real-time knowledge, the model might generate responses that *seem plausible* based on its pattern-matching capabilities, but which are not factually accurate or relevant. While ChatGPT can synthesize information based on patterns it has identified, it does not have the ability to verify the truth or current relevance of the text it generates.

• • •

You must be aware of these limitations and critically evaluate the authenticity and validity of AI-generated content. You should also read the legal authority yourself, to fully understand and determine whether the information provided by ChatGPT applies correctly to the issue at hand.

Similarly, if a generative AI tool provides a summary or an analysis of a case or legal document, you must thoroughly review and understand the case or document and not rely solely on the AI-generated summary or analysis. While generative AI tools can help identify useful authority and provide helpful summaries, you must not outsource the work of reading and understanding the legal authority.

Remember, when you, as a lawyer, sign your name to a pleading or document, you are verifying that the statements and representations made in that document are accurate and factually substantiated to the best of your knowledge, understanding, and belief. Using AI tools to aid in research does not absolve lawyers from their professional responsibility to ensure the validity and appropriateness of the legal arguments presented. This includes ensuring that legal precedents are correctly interpreted and applied, and that the law cited is current and applicable to the jurisdiction and circumstances of the case at hand. Hence, any information derived from generative AI tools such as ChatGPT should be independently verified against original legal sources before it is used in any professional context.

Professional Identity Formation Reflection

Reflect on your understanding of the limitations of generative AI tools such as ChatGPT. How does your current understanding of these limitations influence your use of these tools in your studies?

Can you recall a situation where you had to critically evaluate the authenticity and validity of AI-generated content? How did you ensure the information you used was accurate and relevant?

In the context of your future legal career, how do these practices contribute to your professional identity as a future lawyer who is responsible for verifying the validity and appropriateness of legal arguments?

Consequences of Forgetting That ChatGPT Can Provide False Information or Hallucinate

When lawyers use generative AI models and fail to verify the information those models provide, there can be dire consequences. And many users overlook the potential for false information when using ChatGPT. ChatGPT and similar generative AI tools provide convincing and coherent responses that can lead users to trust the information it provides without critically assessing its accuracy. This false sense of trust means that some users may not take the time to verify the information through external sources before accepting and sharing it. Users also may overestimate the expertise of ChatGPT and similar AI tools, forgetting that the underlying large language models are limited by their training data and may lack access to real-time or up-to-date information.

Lawyers have a professional and ethical obligation to provide accurate and reliable information to their clients, to the court, and to other parties involved in legal matters. If lawyers rely on ChatGPT without fact-checking or critically assessing its responses, they risk basing their arguments, advice, or legal strategies on incorrect or fabricated information. This can lead the lawyer to misrepresent facts, present flawed arguments, or provide erroneous advice, all of which can harm their clients' cases or compromise the integrity of the legal system.

Lawyers have a duty to act in the best interests of their clients and to uphold the principles of honesty, integrity, and professional competence. Relying solely on ChatGPT without critically evaluating its responses or conducting independent research can be seen as a failure to fulfill these ethical responsibilities.

The following case study illustrates the serious professional and legal consequences that can occur when lawyers overlook or underestimate the limitations and potential inaccuracies of AI tools such as ChatGPT.

Case Study: Mata v. Avianca, Inc. (Part II)

As discussed in Chapter 2, *Mata v. Avianca, Inc.*,[2] a case filed in the Southern District of New York, was a personal injury case in which plaintiff Roberto Mata sued the airline Avianca, claiming that he was injured when a metal serving cart struck his knee during a flight to John F. Kennedy International Airport in New York. Counsel for the defendant, Avianca, filed a motion to dismiss. Plaintiff's counsel, Peter LoDuca, filed an opposition to a motion to dismiss with citations to cases the defendant's counsel could not find. When the defendant's counsel called this to the court's attention, the court issued an order requiring Mr. LoDuca to provide an affidavit annexing copies of the in-question judicial opinions cited in his opposition to the motion to dismiss. Mr. LoDuca submitted an affidavit on April 25, 2023, providing citations and attaching copies of court opinions cited in the opposition to a motion to dismiss and declaring that the information in the affidavit was true and correct. However, six of the submitted cases were fabricated by ChatGPT. Although LoDuca was the plaintiff's counsel of record, an attorney in LoDuca's firm, Steven A. Schwartz, was the attorney conducting the research and preparing the pleadings for the case. LoDuca submitted an affidavit on May 25, 2023, admitting that he did not conduct the research or verify the cases he declared to be true and correct in his April 25, 2023, affidavit. Schwartz also submitted an affidavit and admitted that he performed all of the legal research and had used ChatGPT to identify legal authority, later determined by the court to be nonexistent, to support the plaintiff's position in opposition to the motion to dismiss.

On May 26, 2023, the court ordered LoDuca to show cause why he should not be sanctioned for (1) the citation of non-existent cases, (2) the submission to the court of copies of non-existent judicial opinions, and (3) the use of a false and fraudulent notarization in his affidavit filed on April 25, 2023. The court also ordered Schwartz to show cause why he should not be sanctioned and referred to the New York State Bar grievance committee for aiding and causing (1) the citation of non-existent cases, (2) the submission to the court of copies of non-existent judicial opinions, and (3) the use of a false and fraudulent notarization in LoDuca's affidavit filed on April 25, 2023.

A hearing on the order to show cause was held on June 8, 2023. Here is an excerpt from the hearing transcript:[3]

THE COURT: And the question you asked ChatGPT was: Provide case law in support that statute of limitations is tolled by bankruptcy of defendant under the Montreal Convention.
MR. SCHWARTZ: Correct.
THE COURT: And they did that.
MR. SCHWARTZ: Correct.
THE COURT: But I asked you before, did you ever ask them the question, what is the law? Not provide me with a case. The computer complied. It provided you with a case. It wrote a case. It followed your command.

MR. SCHWARTZ: Prior to that, I asked it to argue that the statute of limitations is tolled by the bankruptcy of the defendant pursuant to the Montreal Convention.

THE COURT: What case did they cite to that?

MR. SCHWARTZ: Didn't cite any cases.

THE COURT: Now, there came a time that you were told that Varghese supported the proposition, correct?

MR. SCHWARTZ: Correct.

THE COURT: Did you read Varghese?

MR. SCHWARTZ: I read the excerpts that were produced, yes.

THE COURT: Are you accustomed to citing cases without reviewing the entirety of the text of the case?

MR. SCHWARTZ: No.

THE COURT: Then what caused your departure here?

MR. SCHWARTZ: I just never could imagine that ChatGPT would produce fabricated cases, and my assumption was that I'm using a search engine that's searching sources that I don't have access to, and—mistakenly, and I take full responsibility for it. And looking back, obviously, very extremely regretful that I didn't take those further steps. But due to the newness of the technology and my obvious inexperience in using the technology and my false assumptions as to what this website does, it just never occurred to me that it would be making up cases. I just assumed it was not able to access the full opinions.

THE COURT: But you just said to me, you are not accustomed to citing cases without reviewing the entirety of the case, yet you did not have the entirety of the case, correct?

MR. SCHWARTZ: Correct.

THE COURT: Now, you knew, and you told me this already, that you can obtain the full text of a circuit court case on the Internet. Maybe it doesn't do great research, but if you have the citation to the case, you can pull up that case on the Internet, correct, on Google, correct?

MR. SCHWARTZ: Correct.

THE COURT: Did you say, well they gave me part of Varghese, let me look at the full Varghese decision?

MR. SCHWARTZ: I did.

THE COURT: And what did you find when you went to look up the full Varghese decision?

MR. SCHWARTZ: I couldn't find it.

THE COURT: And yet you cited it in the brief to me.

MR. SCHWARTZ: I did, again, operating under the false assumption and disbelief that this website could produce completely fabricated cases. And if I knew that, I obviously never would have submitted these cases. I obviously should have taken further steps to go and find the Federal Reporter, or go to, more obviously, Westlaw or Lexis and verify that these cases were accurate. In hindsight, God, I wish I did that, and I didn't do it. Again, I had no intent to deceive this Court or the defendants. I was operating under a misconception and a disbelief that these cases could not be real, and that this website is obtaining those cases from some source that I can't get access to. And I did not follow up, and I should have followed up even earlier, and I should have verified it.

On June 22, 2023, the court sanctioned the attorneys $5,000, jointly and severally. The court also ordered the attorneys to send a letter to their client and to each judge falsely identified as the author of the fake opinions, including a copy of the court's opinion and order; a transcript of the June 8, 2023 hearing; and a copy of the April 25, 2023 Affirmation filed by the attorneys.

• • •

This case should serve as a stark reminder of the essential role of due diligence in the practice of law and the importance of understanding and respecting the capabilities and limitations of AI tools. The critical importance of fact-checking, independent research, and the application of professional expertise and judgment cannot be emphasized enough. Lawyers must understand that AI tools are not infallible oracles but are tools that should aid, not replace, their professional judgment and due diligence. Additionally, it underscores the ethical duty of lawyers to ensure the accuracy of the legal authorities they cite and the validity of the arguments they present to the court. Blind trust in AI-generated responses can have damaging professional and legal repercussions, as demonstrated by the sanctions and professional disciplinary proceedings and possible malpractice claims faced by Mr. LoDuca and Mr. Schwartz.

Real-Life Examples of Courts Requiring Attorneys to Verify or Certify Cases Cited

As a consequence of the *Mata v. Avianca, Inc.* case, some judges are requiring attorneys to disclose if they have used AI in the preparation of documents filed with the court and to certify that the cases they cite have been verified.

> *Example 1*: U.S. District Judge Brantley Starr of the Northern District of Texas issued an order on May 30, 2023, that requires all attorneys appearing before his court to certify that no portion of any filing will be drafted by generative AI. The order also requires attorneys to certify that any language drafted by generative AI will be checked for accuracy by a human being.[4]

> *Example 2*: Magistrate Judge Gabriel A. Fuentes of the U.S. District Court for the Northern District of Illinois adopted a standing order on May 31, 2023, providing that "any party using any generative AI tool in the preparation of drafting documents for filing with the Court must disclose in the filing that AI was used" with the disclosure including the specific AI tool and the manner in which it was used.[5]

> *Example 3*: U.S. District Judge Michael Baylson of the Eastern District of Pennsylvania issued a one-line order on June 6, 2023, requiring attorneys and *pro se* litigants to disclose when they have used AI to prepare any court filings and to certify that they have verified the accuracy of any case citations in their filings.[6]

> *Example 4*: U.S. Court of International Trade Judge Stephen A. Vaden issued an order on June 8, 2023, requiring attorneys to disclose the use of generative artificial intelligence tools in their brief writing, citing concerns about not being able to protect confidential or business proprietary information entered into these tools.[7]

Professional Identity Formation Reflection

Reflect on the *Mata v. Avianca, Inc.* case study. How does this case influence your perspective on the role of AI tools in legal research and decision making? How would you integrate the lessons from this case into your professional practice to ensure you fulfill your ethical responsibilities toward your clients, the court, and the integrity of the legal system?

Furthermore, consider the consequences for Mr. LoDuca and Mr. Schwartz. How does their experience influence your understanding of the importance of critical thinking, independent research, and professional judgment in the context of using AI tools in your future legal work?

ENDNOTES

1. "Introducing ChatGPT," OpenAI (blog) November 30, 2022, https://openai.com/blog/chatgpt (see "Limitations").
2. Mata v. Avianca, Inc., No. 1:22-cv-01461, United States District Court, S.D. New York, https://www.courtlistener.com/docket/63107798/mata-v-avianca-inc/.
3. Transcript of Order to Show Cause Hearing at 26-29, Mata v. Avianca, Inc. No. 1:22-cv-01461 (S.D.N.Y. June 8, 2023).
4. Judge Specific Requirements, "Mandatory Certification Regarding Generative Artificial Intelligence," Judge Brantley Starr, United States District Court, Northern District of Texas, May 20, 2023, https://www.txnd.uscourts.gov/judge/judge-brantley-starr.
5. "Standing Order for Civil Cases before Magistrate Judge Fuentes," United States Magistrate Judge Gabriel A. Fuentes, United States District Court, Northern District of Illinois, May 31, 2023, https://www.ilnd.uscourts.gov/_assets/_documents/_forms/_judges/Fuentes/Standing%20Order%20For%20Civil%20Cases%20Before%20Judge%20Fuentes%20rev'd%205-31-23%20(002).pdf.
6. "Standing Order Re: Artificial Intelligence ('AI') in Cases Assigned to Judge Baylson," Judge Michael M. Baylson, United States District Court, Eastern District of Pennsylvania, June 6, 2023, https://www.paed.uscourts.gov/documents/standord/Standing%20Order%20Re%20Artificial%20Intelligence%206.6.pdf.
7. "Order on Artificial Intelligence," Judge Stephen A. Vaden, United States Court of International Trade, June 8, 2023, https://www.internationaltradeinsights.com/wp-content/uploads/sites/610/2023/06/Vaden-Artificial-Intelligence-Order.pdf.

Chapter 4

Use of Generative AI in the Legal Profession

As we've discussed, generative AI tools are being incorporated into legal practice to assist with legal research, analysis, and document drafting. For this reason, it is important for law students (and legal educators) to gain an understanding and appreciation for the state of the legal industry as it relates to generative AI.

To ensure you appreciate the impact generative AI is having on the legal profession, you should

- Become familiar with some of the new generative AI legal products and tools while you are still in law school,
- Seek to understand why some lawyers hesitate to adopt generative AI tools, and
- Gain an understanding of the impact generative AI may have on the access to justice crisis.

LEGAL TOOLS LEVERAGING GENERATIVE AI

Legal product companies are leveraging generative AI technology to create a variety of innovative products that perform legal research, draft legal documents, review contracts, and manage legal data. These generative AI–driven tools, built on powerful language models such as OpenAI's GPT-4, enhance the capabilities of legal practitioners to such a degree that they are reshaping the landscape and workflow of legal practice.

Having law-specific, secure tools addresses some of the privacy concerns over the use of publicly available large language models such as ChatGPT. These AI tools are tailored to the specific needs of the legal profession. They can be trained on domain-specific data and programmed to adhere to strict confidentiality and privacy standards, mitigating the potential risks associated with data privacy violations.

Leading Legal Generative AI Products

The following are some of the leading products in this emerging field. Note, the following descriptions are true as of this writing, but AI is a rapidly developing field. To ensure you have the most current information, you should research these products online.

CoCounsel, *by Casetext*

Casetext released *CoCounsel* in March 2023. CoCounsel is an AI legal assistant powered by OpenAI's GPT-4. CoCounsel uses generative AI to perform a multitude of tasks. It can

- Review of a set of documents to answer a set of questions,
- Review of a set of contracts to answer a set of questions,
- Draft legal memos,
- Prepare deposition questions,
- Review contracts for compliance with policies and guidelines, and
- Summarize documents.

On Monday, June 26, 2023, Thomson Reuters (parent company of Westlaw) announced that it had agreed to acquire Casetext in a $650 million all-cash deal.

AI Assist, *by Ironclad*

Ironclad, a contract management platform, released its generative AI product, *AI Assist*, in February 2023. Also powered by OpenAI's ChatGPT technology, AI Assist can, among other things

- Identify and redline irregularities in contracts,
- Make redline suggestions based on a company's preferred clause and language guidelines, and
- Ensure contract compliance by using a set library of preferred language and clauses.

Lexis+ AI, *by LexisNexis*

In May 2023, LexisNexis announced the launch of *Lexis+ AI,* a generative AI platform that uses GPT-4 and other large language models to assist with legal tasks. In addition to other tasks, Lexis+ AI can

- Answer legal research questions,
- Summarize legal issues, and
- Draft of documents such as demand letters or client emails.

Lexis+ AI also has a conversational search functionality. Because Lexis+ AI uses verified content from LexisNexis research platform databases, there is a significantly lower risk of hallucinations with Lexis+ AI compared with ChatGPT. Lexis+ AI is expected to be released in late summer 2023.

Harvey AI, *by Harvey*

Harvey AI is a legal artificial intelligence platform that is backed by OpenAI and uses OpenAI's ChatGPT technology to answer legal questions and provide guidance across various practice areas, jurisdictions, and legal systems. Harvey AI builds custom large language models for elite law firms to assist with research, drafting of legal documents, contract analysis, due diligence, litigation, and regulatory compliance.

The law firm of Allen & Overy (A&O) announced its partnership with Harvey AI in February 2023, and in March 2023, the large accounting firm PricewaterhouseCoopers LLP (PwC) announced its partnership with Harvey to launch a legal chatbot.

Although still in the early stages of development, Harvey AI has more than 15,000 law firms on its waiting list.

Spellbook, *by Spellbook*

Spellbook, released in 2022, is an AI add-in for Word that helps lawyers draft and review contracts in Word. It is powered by OpenAI's GPT large language model. Spellbook can suggest language, negotiate points, summarize terms, and explain contracts in simple words.

Copilot, *by LawDroid*

LawDroid is a legal technology company that provides AI tools for legal professionals. LawDroid's generative AI product, *Copilot*, is in development as of this writing and is available in beta by request on an early-access basis. Copilot is a virtual legal assistant that uses the natural language processing capabilities of GPT-3.5. Copilot can assist with research, drafting emails and letters, summarizing documents, and brainstorming.

• • •

The rise of generative AI in the legal sector is a paradigm shift that will dramatically alter the way you will approach your work as a legal professional. However, it is important for you to keep in mind that AI is an *assistive* technology, which should complement, not replace, human judgment. As AI technologies continue to evolve, the legal profession can expect further enhancements to these tools, expanding their functionalities and capabilities.

> New generative AI legal products are being developed at a rapid pace. For a current list, see the University of Arizona James E. Rogers College of Law, Daniel F. Cracchiolo Library's *ChatGPT and Bing Chat Generative AI Legal Research Guide*, "New Legal Technology Products Which Utilize ChatGPT Technology."

THE LEGAL PROFESSION'S CAUTIOUS RESPONSE TO ADOPTING GENERATIVE AI TOOLS

Despite the creation of both new and improved AI-enhanced products, the legal profession as a whole is not particularly tech-savvy, and some segments of the legal profession have taken a cautious approach to adopting generative AI tools.

One reason for caution many be the "black box" issue, discussed in Chapter 1. Many AI models, while powerful, operate on algorithms and data inputs that may not always be transparent or easily explainable to attorneys. This lack of transparency and explainability can create challenges in holding AI systems accountable for their outputs and decision-making processes. The legal profession, being deeply committed to ethical conduct and the protection of clients' rights, may be cautious in adopting AI technologies until issues of transparency and accountability are adequately addressed.

The age of lawyers may also be contributing to the slow adoption of technology. According to the American Bar Association's 2022 edition of the Profile of the Legal Profession,

> The median age for lawyers in 2021 was 46.5 years old, which means half were younger and half older. By comparison, the median age of all U.S. workers was 42.2—four years younger than the typical lawyer.

According to the American Bar Association (ABA), there are two reasons the median age for lawyers is older than the median age for other workers.

> First, very few lawyers are younger than 25, [even though] roughly 12% of all American workers are younger than 25. Second, many lawyers work past age 65. Nearly 13% of all lawyers—that's 1 in 8—are 65 or older. Only 7% of all U.S. workers are 65 or older.

Older lawyers, who make up a significant portion of the profession, may have had limited exposure to, or formal training in, emerging technologies during their legal education and early years of practice. This relative unfamiliarity with technology can cause older lawyers to resist change. Many more senior lawyers also resist change because of the perceived challenges associated with learning new skills, especially when they have developed a level of comfort and expertise with their established workflows and practices, even if they are inefficient.

It is important to note that these factors are general observations and may not apply uniformly to all lawyers. Nevertheless, the demographic composition of the legal profession, with its older median age and a higher percentage of lawyers working past the age of 65, can contribute to a level of resistance to change within the profession, including the adoption of new technologies such as generative AI.

However, notwithstanding an attorney's age or comfort level, lawyers are responsible for keeping abreast of changing technologies and obtaining and using technology in an appropriate way consistent with their clients' needs.

The ABA Model Rule of Professional Conduct 1.1, which relates to attorney competence, states that "[a] lawyer shall provide *competent representation* to a client. *Competent representation* requires the legal knowledge, skill, thoroughness and preparation reasonably necessary for the representation."

In 2012, the ABA clarified what is meant by "competent representation" within the context of the rule. The ABA stated in the new Comment 8 of the rule that "[t]o maintain the requisite knowledge and skill, a lawyer should keep abreast of changes in the law and its practice, including the benefits and risks associated with relevant technology, engage in continuing study and education and comply with all continuing legal education requirements to which the lawyer is subject." This amendment emphasized the importance of technology in law practice and lawyers' duty to be technologically competent.

The legal profession, like many other fields, has a generation gap when it comes to technology adoption. Younger lawyers, who often are more tech-savvy and have grown up in a digital age, may be more open to incorporating new technologies, including generative AI, into their legal practice.

As a law student, you should be aware of and understand these dynamics. You will be entering a job market that operates within a tech-influenced legal profession. Recognizing the cautious approach of some attorneys and law firms to adopting generative AI and other emerging technologies will enable you to position yourself strategically for a successful job search and future career. While in law school, you should do the following:

- Seek opportunities to identify and bridge the technology gap in legal practice.
- Stay up-to-date on the latest advancements, develop your technological proficiency, and actively participate in technology-focused educational programs.
- Advocate for the responsible integration of AI technologies in legal practice. By engaging in discussions on ethics, transparency, and accountability, you will help shape the development of guidelines and frameworks that address concerns surrounding generative AI. In this way you can contribute to changing the landscape of legal practice.
- Actively seek out internships, clerkships, or mentorship opportunities in law firms or organizations that are at the forefront of technological advancements. This will give you firsthand experience in leveraging generative AI tools ethically and effectively.
- Commit yourself to learning and to adapting, recognizing that technological advancements will continue to shape the legal profession throughout your career.
- Develop a solid foundation in legal principles (i.e., fundamental concepts and rules that underpin the field of law) and critical thinking skills, which will allow you to understand how AI tools can be applied in a legal context and assess their accuracy and reliability.

By combining your legal expertise with an understanding of generative AI and other emerging technologies,

Be aware that new practice areas are being created to address the legal, ethical, and regulatory challenges posed by emerging technologies such as generative AI.

Generative AI Is the Hot New Practice at Law Firms

you can position yourself as a valuable asset in the tech-influenced legal landscape.

Professional Identity Formation Reflection

Reflect on your personal stance toward the adoption of generative AI in the legal profession. Based on the discussions in this chapter, what factors resonate most with you? How might these factors influence your approach to technology as you enter the legal profession?

Consider how your understanding of the generative AI landscape may inform your professional identity and career choices. How do you anticipate balancing the need for technical proficiency with the preservation of traditional legal principles and practices? How might you contribute to discussions surrounding the ethical implications and accountability issues of AI integration in the legal profession?

HOW GENERATIVE AI MAY IMPACT THE ACCESS TO JUSTICE CRISIS

In addition to being exposed to new generative AI tools and understanding the reasons for its measured adoption, as a law student, you should also recognize the impact that generative AI may have on the access to justice crisis.

The *access to justice crisis* refers to the increasing difficulty that individuals and small businesses, particularly those in marginalized communities or the disadvantaged, face when trying to access the legal system to protect their rights, resolve disputes, or seek redress for grievances. The U.S. ranks 115th out of 140 countries for accessibility and affordability of legal services according to the World Justice Project's 2022 Rule of Law Index. Here are some additional staggering facts:

- More than a hundred million Americans encounter civil justice problems annually, yet a large majority of them go without legal aid.[1]
- Low-income Americans do not receive any or enough legal help for 92 percent of their civil legal problems.[2]
- About 60 percent of small business owners with significant legal problems lack legal representation.[3]
- In 76 percent of state court civil cases, at least one party is unrepresented.[4]

According to the Legal Services Corporation's (LSC) 2022 Justice Gap Study, common civil legal problems among low-income households often relate to health, finances, rental housing, children, custody, education, income maintenance, and disability. Although the LSC report focuses on low-income households, middle-class households struggle to secure legal advice and representation in many of these same areas.

There are several reasons for this civil legal services justice crisis. In her article, "What We Know and Need to Know About the Legal Needs of the Public," Rebecca Sandefur notes that many people fail to even recognize that their problems call for legal assistance.[5] Even when people understand that they may need legal counsel or advice, many may not fully appreciate the significance of that need and the consequences of not receiving legal advice and taking action. There is a tremendous lack of trust in lawyers, Sandefur notes, which causes individuals to forgo seeking assistance from a lawyer. And, not surprisingly, many do not seek legal assistance because they cannot afford the services of lawyers.

Efforts to address the access to justice crisis are varied and ongoing, but the justice gap is widening. In 2017, the LSC reported that 86 percent of the civil legal problems reported by low-income households received inadequate or no legal help. That number increased to *92 percent* in 2022.

Legal aid and pro bono work by lawyers are traditional responses, but these solutions alone are insufficient to meet the scale of the crisis. Increasingly, attention is turning to systemic reforms and innovations, such as simplifying legal processes, leveraging technology to provide legal services, and expanding the roles of paralegals and other non-lawyer professionals.

Many who are working to end the access to justice gap are wondering if generative AI tools can provide meaningful assistance to those who have no choice but to represent themselves. There are several legal technology platforms that provides online services and resources for those wishing or needing to represent themselves in court. However, these platforms do not, and are prohibited from, providing legal advice.

For example, Courtroom5, one of the legal technology platforms, provides its users, who are self-represented individuals and small businesses, with information, training, and tools to manage their cases, from crafting motions and drafting pleadings to tracking their cases' progress.

However, Courtroom5 cannot provide legal advice about the user's specific situation. And while Courtroom5 can aid the user by providing general information for crafting legal arguments, referencing existing laws, and creating legal documents to file in court, Courtroom5 does not answer specific legal questions. Individuals who are unable to secure legal representation find themselves having to navigate the very complex world of litigation without any legal advice about their own case.

Generative AI has the potential to play a significant role in helping *pro se* litigants (i.e., those representing themselves) in court. It can act as a legal advisor, offering basic legal information and advice in response to a user's queries. Generative AI can also assist in the drafting of legal documents.

However, it's important to remember that while generative AI can be a helpful tool for *pro se* litigants, it is not a complete replacement for a human lawyer. AI can provide information and support, but, as we have discussed, AI does not possess the full range of skills and expertise of a human legal professional. AI lacks the ability to provide emotional support, to understand the subtleties of a situation beyond the facts, and to advocate in court. Therefore, while generative AI can help bridge the gap, and may be part of the solution to the access to justice crisis, it is not the entire solution.

Exercise

The ABA requires law schools to provide substantial opportunities for students to participate in pro bono legal services. In explaining this requirement, the ABA notes that the ABA Model Rules of Professional Conduct encourages lawyers to provide pro bono legal services each year. The ABA further states that law schools are encouraged to promote opportunities for law students to provide at least 50 hours of pro bono service over their law school career.

Determine the pro bono opportunities your law school provides. Does your school have a minimum pro bono hour requirement? If so, what is it? If not, does your school encourage the completion of a certain number of pro bono hours by students? Look up the pro bono guidance in the state where you plan to practice. What is the requirement or preference?

Professional Identity Formation Reflection

As future lawyers, it's crucial for law students to understand the scope and scale of the access to justice crisis. Not only does it present a significant challenge to the functioning of the legal system, but it also raises profound questions about the nature of justice itself. The role of lawyers extends beyond the courtroom or the law firm; it involves a commitment to ensuring that the legal system serves all individuals fairly and equitably. Addressing the access to justice crisis is not just a matter of policy—it's a fundamental aspect of the professional responsibility future lawyer will bear.

Prior to this reading, were you aware of the access to justice crisis? What are your thoughts regarding what law students and lawyers should know about the access to justice crisis? Every law school encourages students and every state encourages lawyers to complete pro bono hours.

Think about the type of pro bono work you would like to engage in as a law student. As you think about the pro bono work you will do, ask yourself the following questions:

- How might your law school pro bono work help promote justice and equality in the legal system?
- How might your law school pro bono experience foster empathy, compassion, and a sense of social responsibility, traits that are valuable for any legal professional?
- How might your law school pro bono work help instill the value of volunteering and demonstrate a commitment to upholding the profession's ideals?
- How might your law school pro bono work provide you with practical experience that can supplement your classroom learning and help you become a better-prepared lawyer upon graduation?
- How might your law school pro bono work help you develop essential lawyering skills such as client counseling, negotiation, research, writing, and advocacy?

• • •

Generative AI is gradually making its mark on the legal profession, enhancing research, analysis, drafting, and overall workflow with innovative products such as CoCounsel. However, adoption has been measured due to factors such as the profession's reliance on professional judgment and ethical standards and its rootedness in tradition and precedent. The legal profession's demographic composition and perceived risks associated with new technologies also contribute to this cautious approach. Hence, law students need to understand these dynamics as well as the impact of generative AI on the access to justice crisis. By embracing continuous learning and adaptability, advocating for the responsible integration of AI technologies, and leveraging the benefits of generative AI, law students can help shape the future of a tech-influenced legal profession and improve access to justice.

ENDNOTES

1. Ralph Baxter, "Dereliction of Duty: State-Bar Inaction in Response to America's Access-to-Justice Crisis," *Yale Law Journal* 132 (October 19, 2022): 228, 230. https://www.yalelawjournal.org/pdf/F7.BaxterFinalDraftWEB_jwg5p1p3.pdf.
2. "The 2022 Justice Gap Study," Legal Services Corporation (LSC), accessed June 30, 2023, https://justicegap.lsc.gov/the-report/.
3. Baxter, "Dereliction of Duty," 228, 230.
4. "The Landscape of Civil Litigation in State Courts," Civil Justice Initiative, National Center for State Courts, November 11, 2015, https://www.ncsc.org/__data/assets/pdf_file/0020/13376/civiljusticereport-2015.pdf.
5. Rebecca L. Sandefur, "What We Know and Need to Know About the Legal Needs of the Public," *South Carolina Law Review* 67, no. 2 (Winter 2016): 443, 448-450. https://scholarcommons.sc.edu/sclr/vol67/iss2/16.